THEY GAVE US AMERICA

THEY GAVE US AMERICA

Rhoda Hoff and Phyllis Moir

THE WESTMINSTER PRESS

PHILADELPHIA

STANDARD BOOK NO. 664-32442-8

LIBRARY OF CONGRESS CATALOG CARD NO. 69-15249

Grateful acknowledgment is made to the following for permission to use their copyrighted material:

The Bodley Head Ltd., for excerpts from *The Diary of Thomas Turner of East Hoathly,* edited by Florence Marie Turner.

Alfred A. Knopf, Inc., for the excerpt from William Bradford's *Of Plymouth Plantation,* edited by Samuel Eliot Morison.

Meredith Press: for excerpts from *Diary of a Surgeon in the Years 1751–1752,* edited by Ernest Gray, copyright 1937, D. Appleton-Century Company, Inc.; for excerpts from *Diary of a Young Lady of Fashion in the Years 1764–1765,* by Cleone Knox. Copyright, 1926, by Magdalen King-Hall; copyright renewed 1953.

Francis T. P. Plimpton, for excerpts from *The Education of Shakespeare,* by George A. Plimpton, published by Oxford University Press, 1933.

G. P. Putnam's Sons, for excerpts from *The Chamberlain Letters,* edited by Elizabeth Thomson. Copyright © 1965 by G. P. Putnam's Sons.

BOOK DESIGN
by
VERA MCKINLEY

PUBLISHED BY THE WESTMINSTER PRESS®

PHILADELPHIA, PENNSYLVANIA

PRINTED IN THE UNITED STATES OF AMERICA

CONTENTS

This portrait of Sir Walter Raleigh, which appeared in 1617 in *The History of the World*, was the only one published during his lifetime.

1

QUEEN ELIZABETH I GRANTS A CHARTER

1584

Sir Walter Raleigh, son of a Devon squire, Oxford student, gallant soldier, poet, and captain of the Queen's Guard, was granted the first charter "to explore and colonise barbarous lands in the New World." At his own expense he financed no fewer than three separate expeditions: one in 1584 led by Amadas and Barlowe; another in 1585 under the direction of Grenville and Lane; and, finally, one in 1587 captained by John White. Unfortunately, however, the time was not yet ripe for colonization and although Raleigh's men planted a colony on Roanoke Island at the entrance to Pamlico Sound in what is now the State of North Carolina, the venture ended in frustration and failure.

Raleigh's charter was the first of its kind. Whereas he and his heirs were granted full powers to protect and defend any colonies they might plant, Queen Elizabeth reserved for herself the allegiance of her future subjects as well as "the fifth part of all the ore of gold and silver there obtained after such discovery."

"FOR EVER HOLDEN BY W. RALEIGH"

On March 25th, 1584 Walter Raleigh was given a charter which empowered "Our trusty and well-beloved servant Walter Raleigh, Esquire, his heirs and assigns to discover such remote heathen and barbarous lands, not actually possessed by any Christian prince, nor inhabited by Christian people, as to him or them shall seem good, to hold the same with all prerogatives, commodities, jurisdictions, royalties and privileges, by sea and land, as We by letters patents, may grant, or any of Our progenitors have granted: with licence to inhabit or remain, build and fortify, at the discretion of the said W. Raleigh, his heirs, etc., the statutes or acts against fugitives, or such as depart this realm unprivileged, notwithstanding. We likewise grant him or them full power to take or lead such of Our subjects as shall willingly accompany him or them; also to employ and use sufficient shipping and furniture for transportation and navigation in that behalf. Further that the said W. Raleigh and his heirs shall enjoy for ever all the soil of such lands, or towns in the same, with the rights and royalties, as well marine as other, within the said land or seas adjoining, with full power to dispose thereof according to the laws of England, at his and their will, to any person within the allegiance of Us or Our heirs, reserving always to Us, for all service, duties, and demands, the fifth part of all the ore of gold and silver there obtained after such discovery. All which lands and countries shall be for ever holden by the said W. Raleigh, his heirs, etc., by homage, and by the said payment reserved only for all services.

We likewise grant to the said Raleigh and his heirs licence for their defence, to repel by land or sea all persons that shall without his or their liking attempt to inhabit the said Countries, or within two hundred leagues of the places in them where he or they within six years next ensuing shall make their dwellings, if not before inhabited by the subjects of any Christian prince in amity with Us; giving also power to him or them to take those persons, with their ships and goods, and keep them as lawful prize, who without his or their licence shall be found trafficking within the limits aforesaid, Our subjects and others in amity with Us only excepted. And as well for uniting in more perfect league such Countries with Our realms of England and Ireland, as for the encouragement of men to their enterprises, We declare that all such Countries so possessed shall be of Our allegiance.

And We grant to the said Walter Raleigh, his heirs, and to all being of Our allegiance whose names shall be entered in some Court of Record within our realm of England, who with the assent of the said W. Raleigh, his heirs, etc. shall in his journeys for discovery or conquest hereafter travel to such lands, that they and every [one] of them, being either born within Our said realms of England or Ireland, or any other place within Our allegiance, and who shall hereafter be inhabitants of any of the lands aforesaid; shall have the privileges of free denizens and persons native of England, in such ample manner as if they were born and personally resident in Our said realm of England, any law, custom, or usage notwithstanding. And further, for the safety of all that shall adventure themselves, We grant the said Walter Raleigh, and his heirs, full power and authority within the said lands, in the way by the seas thither, and from thence, to correct, punish, pardon, govern by their good discretions and policies, as well in cause capital or criminal, as civil, both marine and other, all Our subjects who so adventure themselves and shall inhabit the territories aforesaid, or shall abide within two hundred leagues of any such places where he or they shall inhabit within six years next ensuing, according to such Statutes as shall be by him or them established; so that the said Statutes of Laws conform as near as conveniently may be with those of England, and also so as they be not against the Christian faith, or any way withdraw the people of those lands from Our allegiance.

2

A LOVER REQUESTS HIS LADY'S LOVE

1568

When William Shakespeare was a boy, one of the most popular textbooks used in the grammar schools was William Fulwood's Enemie of Idlenesse, *the first edition of which appeared in 1568.*

The Elizabethan period is known as the golden age of English literature, and the works of genius by Shakespeare, Marlowe, Ben Jonson, Sir Walter Raleigh, and Sir Francis Bacon have enriched the lives of all English-speaking people. Probably there is no more precious legacy inherited by the American colonies from the mother country.

The two letters that follow are taken from Fulwood's book. Although typical of the romantic times in which they were written, they have now become period pieces in more senses than one. In these days the coyness of the lady's answer to the flowery appeal addressed to her by her suitor seems hardly credible. Rules of rhetoric have changed less than social mores.

I. A LOVER REQUESTS HIS LADY'S LOVE

Considering (my sovereign joy) the great virtues of nobility, beauty, and courtesy, wherewith nature by superabundant measure hath in such sort decorated you, that above all other terrestrial bodies you are judged by common voice to obtain the Crown and principality; and on the other side weighing the want and insufficiency of my former services towards you, my trembling hand is scarce able to hold the pen, neither dareth my stammering tongue express that which the afflicted heart through ardent appetite desireth to manifest unto you. Yet Love (which above all animated creatures, holdeth in his domination my inflamed mind) doth so exceed, that it giveth me doubtful boldness, to take in hand to open unto you the secrets of my breast: which is to ask you to understand, that ever since mine eyes did speculate and behold your great beauty, my heart hath remained so bound and entangled, that of its own free will it hath chosen to be included in your sweet prison. By reason whereof, and seeing the vexations and grievous passions of my languishing corpse, caused through the sweet regard of your eyes, and augmented by the great eclipsation of your absence, I am constrained to demand your aid and succour. And because you are she, who only and none other, may send remedy in this case, I therefore most humbly pray and request you, that even as in all other virtues you are sovereign, so likewise in this matter you would show yourself charitable and pitifull. And since you are the cause of this so great and grievous martyrdom, and that you only may help and remedy it, extend therefore the true remedy, by sending a benign answer, the which I most effectuously desire and attend.

II. THE ANSWER OF HIS LADY

My troubled thought so discordeth from your fond affection, that I cannot marvel enough to imagine what cause moved you, and gave you such presumptious boldness, as to trouble and interrupt me of mine accustomed rest, through your abombinable letters and wanton words. Your said letters, (to the end that they should not come into the hands of any other person) I have received: and beholding the contents thereof, with great pain could I bridle mine ire, and withold myself from tearing them in pieces: but considering that such fault is not to be imputed unto the letters which are insensible, but unto the composer and doer of them, I therefore refrained myself from that purpose, willing to exercise mine anger and rigour upon the messenger: but likewise for report's sake, I refrained, from giving him special charge, not thenceforth to return unto me with any such message. And to the end that you shall not presume to continue any longer in this suit, understand that I am not she, unto whom such abusive letters should be sent. I have thought good (contrary to mine accustomed manner) to write unto you at this present, which my spirit with much ado can scarce abide to finish, through the great offence that it feeleth: certifying you, that if you persevere any longer in this matter, you shall do unto me a most displeasant thing, and unto yourself shall purchase great and evident damage. Wherefore I pray you (for the avoiding of all these inconveniences) that you will condescend unto my request: and so doing you shall do me a singular pleasure.

3

AN AUDIENCE WITH QUEEN ELIZABETH I

1598

At the time Paul Hentzner, a traveler from Germany, paid his visit to "Good Queen Bess," she was sixty-five years old and at the height of her power. After defeating the Spanish Armada in 1588, Elizabeth had not only won for England the supremacy of the seas but also for herself the love and admiration of her subjects.

England in 1598 was expanding her commerce in all directions. The peace that Queen Elizabeth had done so much to preserve and promote was freeing her country to march forward in ever-growing prosperity. Great inventions and discoveries gave England the leading role in naval affairs as well as in colonial expansion and commercial prosperity that was to be hers until the mid-twentieth century.

PAUL HENTZNER'S JOURNEY INTO ENGLAND

Upon taking the Air down the River, the first Thing that struck us, was the Ship of that noble Pirate, Sir Francis Drake, in which he is said to have surrounded this Globe of Earth. On the left hand lies Ratcliffe, a considerable Suburb.

We arrived next at the Royal Palace of Greenwich, reported to have been originally built by Humphrey, Duke of Gloucester, and to have received very magnificent Additions from Henry VII. It was here Elizabeth, the present queen, was born, and here she generally resides; particularly in Summer, for the Delightfulness of its Situation. We were admitted into the Presence-Chamber, hung with rich Tapestry, and the Floor after the English Fashion, strewed with Hay [he probably means Rushes], through which the Queen commonly passes in her way to Chapel. At the Door stood a Gentleman dressed in Velvet, with a Gold Chain, whose Office was to introduce to the Queen any Person of Distinction, that came to wait on her. It was Sunday, when there is usually the greatest Attendance of Nobility. In the same Hall were the Archbishop of Canterbury, the Bishop of London, a great number of Councellors of State, Officers of State, Officers of the Crown, and Gentlemen, who waited the Queen's coming out, which she did from her own Apartment, when it was Time to go to Prayers, attended in the following manner:

First went Gentlemen, Barons, Earls, Knights of the Garter, all richly dressed and bareheaded; next came the Chancellor, bearing the Seals in a red Silk Purse, between two: One of which carried the Royal Sceptre, the other the Sword of State, in a red scabbard, studded with golden Fleurs de Lis, the Point upwards. Next came the Queen, in the Sixty-fifth year of her Age, as we were told, very Majestic; her Face oblong, fair, but wrinkled; her Eyes small, yet black and pleasant; her Nose a little hooked; her Lips narrow, and her Teeth black (a Defect the English seem subject to, from their too great Use of Sugar); she had in her Ears two Pearls, with very rich Drops; she wore false Hair, and that red; upon her Head she had a small Crown, reported to be of some of the Gold of the celebrated Lunebourg Table. Her Bosom was uncovered, as all the English Ladies have it, till they marry; and she had on a Necklace of exceeding fine Jewels; her Hands were small, her Fingers long and her Stature neither tall nor low; her Air was stately, her manner of speaking mild and obliging. That Day she was dressed in white Silk bordered with Pearls of the Size of Beans, and over it a Mantle of black Silk, shot with silver Threads; her Train was very long, the end of it borne by a Marchioness; instead of a Chain, she had an oblong Collar of Gold and Jewels. As she went along in all this State and Magnificence, she spoke very graciously, first to one then to another, whether foreign Ministers, or those who attended for different Reasons, in English, French and Italian; for, besides being well-skilled in Greek, Latin and the Languages I have mentioned, she is Mistress of Spanish, Scotch and Dutch. Whoever speaks to her, it is kneeling; now and then she raises some with her Hand. While we were there, a Bohemian Baron, had letters to present to her; and she, after pulling off her Glove, gave him her right Hand to kiss, sparkling with Rings and Jewels, a Mark of particular Favor. Wherever she turned her Face, as she was going along, everybody fell down on their knees.

The Ladies of the Court followed next to her, very handsome and well-shaped, and for the most part dressed in white. She was guarded on each Side by the Gentlemen Pensioners, fifty in Number, with gilt Battleaxes. In the Ante-chapel next the Hall where we were, Petitions were presented to her, and she received them most graciously, which occasioned the Acclamation of, "Long live Queen Elizabeth." She answered it with, "I thank you my good People." In the Chapel was excellent Music; as soon as it and the Service was over, which scarce exceeded half an Hour, the Queen returned in the same State and Order, and prepared to go to Dinner. But while she was still at Prayers, we saw her Table set out with the following Solemnity.

A Gentleman entered the Room bearing a Rod, and along with him another who had a Tablecloth, which after they had both kneeled three Times, with the utmost veneration, he spread upon the Table, and after kneeling again, they both retired. Then came two others, one with the Rod again, the other with a Salt-seller, a Plate and Bread. When they had kneeled, as the others had done, and placed what was brought upon the Table, they too retired with the same Ceremonies performed by the first. At last came an unmarried Lady (we were told she was a Countess), and along with her a married one bearing a Tasting-knife; the former was dressed in white Silk, who, when she had prostrated herself three Times, in the most graceful Manner, approached the Table, and rubbed the Plates with Bread and Salt, with as much Awe as if the Queen had been present. When they had waited there a little while, the Yeomen of the Guard entered, bareheaded, clothed in Scarlet, with a golden Rose upon their Backs, bringing in at each Turn a Course of twenty-four Dishes, served in Plate most of it Gilt. These Dishes were received by a Gentleman in the same Order they were brought, and placed upon the Table, while the Lady taster gave to each of the Guard a mouthful to eat, of the particular Dish he had brought, for Fear of any Poison.

During the Time that this Guard, which consists of the tallest and stoutest Men that can be found in all England, being carefully selected for this Service, were bringing Dinner, twelve Trumpets, and two Kettledrums made the Hall ring for half an Hour together. At the End of this Ceremonial a number of unmarried Ladies appeared, who, with particular Solemnity, lifted the Meat off the Table, and conveyed it into the Queen's inner and more private Chamber, where, after she had chosen for herself, the rest goes to the Ladies of the Court.

The Queen dines and sups alone with very few Attendants; and it is very seldom that anybody, Foreigner or Native, is admitted at that Time, and then only at the Intercession of somebody in Power.

4

THE GUNPOWDER PLOT

1605

The Protestant King James I had hardly ascended the throne in 1603 when plots were hatched against him. The most famous of these is known as the Gunpowder Plot. A small group of wealthy Catholic noblemen, bitterly angry at the new king's lack of toleration for their religious principles, banded together to blow up the Houses of Parliament on November 5, 1605. On this date King James, accompanied by the queen and their eldest son, was scheduled to open Parliament with a joint session of the Lords and Commons. The conspirators had planted barrels of gunpowder in a cellar directly beneath the hall where Parliament was to meet.

The plot misfired. James was warned in time. On the evening of November 4, 1605, the authorities raided the cellar and arrested Guy Fawkes, a veteran Catholic soldier who had been entrusted with the job of setting off the explosives.

Ever since then the children of England celebrate November 5 as Guy Fawkes Day by building enormous bonfires, wearing grotesque masks, and chanting a ragged little rhyme:

Remember, remember the Fifth of November
　Gunpowder treason and plot,
I see no reason why gunpowder treason
　Should ever be forgot.

The following letter was written by John Chamberlain, a famous gossip of the period, to his protégé Dudley Carlton, an employee of one of the suspected conspirators.

NOV. 7, 1605

Though I looked for you before this time, and have often wished you here among your old schoolfellows that are almost all come up to the Parliament, yet as matters are lately fallen out about your Lord, I am well content you be absent.

Not that your Lord [Henry Percy, ninth Earl of Northumberland] as I hope, can be any way touched with this devilish conspiracy, but that nearness of name, blood, long and inward dependence, and familiarity, cannot but leave some aspersion that will not easily or lightly be washed off without time; in which consideration I hear he is rather wished than willed to keep his house.

I cannot but remember what you have diverse times told me touching Thomas Percy [one of the Gunpowder Plot conspirators, and a cousin of the Earl of Northumberland] that you suspected him to be a subtle, flattering, dangerous knave. He hath not only verified your judgement but exceeded all degrees of comparison and gone beyond Nero and Caligula that wished all Rome but one head that they might cut it off at a stroke; for he at one blow would have ruined the whole realm.

He had hired the house or lodging next to the Parliament, together with the cellar or vault under the Upper House, into which by the means of one Johnson [the assumed name of Guy Fawkes] his man—a superstitious papist, or rather a priest as is thought—he hath conveyed any time this twelvemonth as much powder in satchels, as four or five and thirty barrels, hogsheads and firkins could contain, with intent the first day of the Parliament, when the King should be in his speech, to blow them all up, and had so cunningly covered them with billets, faggots, and such trash that without long search they could not be discovered. And but that God blinded him or some of his to send this enclosed [copy of the anonymous warning sent to Lord Monteagle] it was very like to take effect.

But the carrying of it to the Lord of Salisbury and so to the King, it gave such light that, watch being set, the fellow was taken making his trains at midnight with a blind lantern, and presently confessed the plot, yet with such show of resolution that he seemed to be chiefly grieved that it had wanted success. The next day he was carried to the Tower, but what Sir William Waad and other examiners have wrang out of him I cannot learn. Only I hear Sir Edward Bainham, come lately out of the Low Countries, is sought for, and some five or six Jesuits and priests taken in a privy search.

Percy, coming up on a sleeveless errand, and before he was looked for, to your Lord, durst not tarry to see the event but went away that night that his man was taken. . . .

On Tuesday at night we had great ringing and as great store of bonfires as ever I think was seen.

5

THE PERSECUTION OF THE PILGRIMS

1608

In 1593 the English Parliament passed a law forbidding any person to worship God outside the Established Church of England. William Bradford, author of the excerpt that follows, was a member of a small group of dissenters who lived at Scrooby in Nottinghamshire. This small congregation longed to worship God according to their own convictions and they thought that the Church of England must be purged of its "Papist practices."

In 1608 one hundred and twenty-five members of the Scrooby congregation, among them William Bradford, escaped to Holland. The Nottingham authorities had begun to enforce a law against them, inflicting heavy penalties for its defiance. This law stated that no one could go out of the kingdom without a royal license. In Holland there was freedom for all men.

The previous year some of the Scrooby congregation had made their first attempt to flee England. Although this first effort ended in failure, later attempts proved more successful. For some years this band of Pilgrims lived in Leyden, Holland. Then the difficulties of making a living in a foreign country, coupled with the unwillingness of the group to see their children becoming more Dutch than English made them decide to make still another move.

James I had succeeded Queen Elizabeth. Wanting to bring up their children as Englishmen, the Pilgrims decided to migrate to the New World, where they could keep their community intact, worship God according to their faith, and still remain subjects of the English king.

On September 16, 1620, 102 of the company boarded the Mayflower *and set sail for the New World, landing two months later at Plymouth, Massachusetts, and founding there the Pilgrim settlement in America.*

When by the travail and diligence of some godly and zealous preachers, many became enlightened by the Word of God and had their ignorance and sins discovered unto them, and began by His grace to reform their lives and make conscience of their ways; the work of God was no sooner manifest in them but presently they were both scoffed and scorned by the profane multitude; and the ministers urged with the yoke of subscription, or else must be silenced. And the poor people were so vexed with pursuivants [officers of the Church of England whose duty was to enforce conformity] and the commissary courts, as truly their afflictions were not small. Which, notwithstanding they bore sundry years with much patience, till they were occasioned by the continuance and increase of these troubles, and other means which the Lord raised up in those days, to see further into things by the light of the Word of God. How not only these base and beggarly ceremonies were unlawful, but also that the lordly and tyrannous power of the prelates ought not to be submitted unto.

So many, therefore of these professors [as used by Bradford "professor" merely meant one who professed Christianity] as saw the evil of these things and whose hearts the Lord had touched with heavenly zeal for His truth, shook off this yoke of antichristian bondage, and as the Lord's free people joined themselves into a church estate in the fellowship of the gospel, to walk in all His ways made known to them, according to their best endeavours, the Lord assisting them. And that it cost them something this ensuing history will declare.

But after these things they could not long continue in any peaceable condition, but were hunted and persecuted on every side, so that their former afflictions were but as flea-bitings in comparison of those which now came upon them. For some were taken and clapped up in prison, others had their houses beset and watched night and day, and hardly escaped their hands; and the most were fain to flee and leave their houses and habitations, and the means of their livelihood.

Seeing themselves thus molested, and that there was no hope of their continuance there, by a joint consent they resolved to go into the Low Countries, where they heard was freedom of religion for all men. So after they had continued together about a year and kept their meetings every Sabbath in one place or other, exercising the worship of God amongst themselves, notwithstanding all the diligence and malice of their adversaries, they seeing they could no longer continue in that condition they resolved to get over into Holland as they could. Which was in the year 1607 and 1608.

There was a large company of them purposed to get passage at Boston in Lincolnshire, and for that end hired a ship wholly to themselves and made agreement with the master to be ready at a certain day, and take them and their goods in at a convenient place, where they accordingly would all attend in readyness. So after long waiting and large expenses, though he kept not day with them, yet he came at length and took them in, in the night. But when he had them and their goods aboard, he betrayed them, having beforehand plotted with the searchers and other officers so to do; who took them and put them into open boats, and there rifled and ransacked them, searching to their shirts for money, yea even the women; and then carried them back into town and made them a spectacle and wonder to the multitude which came flocking on all sides to behold them. Being thus first, by these catchpoll officers rifled and stripped of their money, books and much other goods, they were presented to the magistrates, and so they were committed to ward. After a month's imprisonment the greatest part were dismissed and sent to the places from whence they came; but seven of the principals were still kept in prison and bound over to the assizes.

The next spring after, there was another attempt made by some of these and others to get over at another place. And it so fell out that they happened upon a Dutchman at Hull, having a ship of his own. They made agreement with him, and acquainted him with their condition, hoping to find more faithfulness in him than in the former of their own nation. He was by appointment to take them in between Grimsby and Hull, where was a large common a good way distant from any town. Now against the prefixed time, the women and children with the goods were sent to the place in a small bark which they had hired for that end; and the men were to meet them by land. But it so fell out that they were there a day before the ship came, and the sea being rough and the women very sick, prevailed with the seamen to put into a creek hard by where they lay on ground at low water. The next morning the ship came but they were fast and could not stir until about noon. In the meantime, the shipmaster, perceiving how the matter was, sent his boat to be getting the men aboard whom he saw ready, walking about the shore. But after the first boatful was got aboard and she was ready to go for more, the master espied a great company, both horse and foot, with guns and other weapons, for the company was raised to take them. The Dutchman, seeing that, swore his country's oath *sacremente*, and having the wind fair, weighed his anchor, hoisted sails, and away.

But the poor men which were got aboard were in great distress for their wives and children which they saw thus to be taken, and were left destitute of their help; and themselves also, not having a cloth to shift them with, more than they had on their backs, and some scarce a penny about them, all they had being aboard the bark. It drew tears from their eyes, and anything they had they would have given to have been ashore again. And afterward they endured a fearful storm at sea, being fourteen days or more before which they arrived at their port.

But to return to the others where we left. The rest of the men that were in greatest danger made shift to escape away before the troop could surprise them, those only staying that best might be assistant unto the women. But pitiful it was to see the heavy case of these poor women in distress; what weeping and crying on every side, some of their husbands that were carried away in the ship as is before related; others not knowing what should become of them and their little ones; others again melted in tears, seeing their poor little ones hanging about them, crying for fear and quaking with cold. Being thus apprehended, they were hurried from one place to another and from one justice to another, till in the end they knew not what to do with them; for to imprison so many women and innocent children for no other cause but that they must go with their husbands, seemed unreasonable and all would cry out of them. And to send them home again was as difficult; for they alleged, as the truth was, they had no homes to go to, for they had either sold or otherwise disposed of their houses and livings. To be short, after they had been thus turmoiled a good while and conveyed from one constable to another, they were glad to be rid of them in the end upon any terms, for all were wearied and tired of them.

But that I be not tedious in these things, I will omit the rest. Yet I may not omit the fruit that came hereby, for by these so public troubles in so many eminent places their cause became famous and occasioned many to look into the same, and their Godly carriage and Christian behaviour was such as left a deep impression in the minds of many. And though some few shrunk at these first conflicts (as it was no marvel) yet many more came on with fresh courage and greatly animated others. And in the end, notwithstanding all these storms of opposition, they all got over at length, some at one time and some at another, and some in one place and some in another, and met together again according to their desires, with no small rejoicing.

6

KING JAMES I AND THE BIBLE

1611

Perhaps the most important and enduring achievement that marked the reign of James I is the Bible that was named after him. Until then the Scriptures had not been widely read. But the publication of the new Bible in 1611 created widespread interest among the common people. When in 1612 a version small enough to be held in the hand made its appearance, humble folk throughout the country for the first time were able to read the Book of Books by the flickering light of their fireplaces.

The effect on the English people of this exposure to the Bible cannot be overestimated. It influenced the writing and speaking of the English language. In encouraging men to think for themselves and to rise in protest against their oppressors, it brought about the downfall of a monarchy.

Cromwell preferred the King James Bible. George Fox and Bunyan used it. In America, Increase and Cotton Mather, as well as John Wesley, true to their English literary heritage, also were devoted to it. Though there are many different religious sects, this great Bible translation, on which fifty-four of the most learned men in England collaborated for the glory of God, king, and country, is still highly respected.

THE GOSPEL ACCORDING TO ST. LUKE, CHAPTER 15, VERSES 11-32.

And he said, A certain man had two sons: And the younger of them said to his father, Father, give me the portion of goods that falleth to me. And he divided unto them his living.

And not many days after the younger son gathered all together, and took his journey into a far country, and there wasted his substance with riotous living.

And when he had spent all, there arose a mighty famine in that land; and he began to be in want.

And he went and joined himself to a citizen of that country; and he sent him into his fields to feed swine.

And he would fain have filled his belly with the husks that the swine did eat: and no man gave unto him.

And when he came to himself, he said, How many hired servants of my father's have bread enough and to spare, and I perish with hunger!

I will arise and go to my father, and will say unto him, Father, I have sinned against heaven, and before thee, And am no more worthy to be called thy son: make me as one of thy hired servants.

And he arose, and came to his father. But when he was yet a great way off, his father saw him, and had compassion, and ran, and fell on his neck, and kissed him.

And the son said unto him, Father, I have sinned against heaven, and in thy sight, and am no more worthy to be called thy son.

But the father said to his servants, Bring forth the best robe, and put it on him; and put a ring on his hand, and shoes on his feet: And bring hither the fatted calf, and kill it; and let us eat, and be merry: For this my son was dead, and is alive again; he was lost, and is found.

And they began to be merry.

Now his elder son was in the field: and as he came and drew nigh to the house, he heard music and dancing.

And he called one of the servants, and asked what these things meant.

And he said unto him, Thy brother is come; and thy father hath killed the fatted calf, because he hath received him safe and sound.

And he was angry, and would not go in: therefore came his father out, and entreated him.

And he answering said to his father, Lo, these many years do I serve thee, neither transgressed I at any time thy commandment; and yet thou never gavest me a kid, that I might make merry with my friends: But as soon as this thy son was come, which hath devoured thy living with harlots, thou hast killed for him the fatted calf.

And he said unto him, Son, thou art ever with me, and all that I have is thine. It was meet that we should make merry, and be glad: for this thy brother was dead, and is alive again; and was lost, and is found.

7

ADMISSION TO CAMBRIDGE COLLEGE 1624

The following letters give a picture of the regal state in which a young nobleman-student came to Cambridge University in the year 1624. On the other hand, Prince Charles, heir to the throne of Britain, arrived at Cambridge in 1967 with one companion, driving his own mini-car!

Lord Thomas Howard, Earl of Arundel and Surrey, whose son, Lord Maltravers, desired to sample the scholar's life, was one of the great noblemen of his time. He is remembered chiefly today as the collector of the famous ancient sculptures known as the Arundel marbles.

To The Right Wor[ll] Mr. Doctor Gwinne
Master of St. John's College in Cambridge

May it please you Mr. Doctor Gwinne

My Lord Arundel having an intent that my Lord Maltravers, his son, and Mr. William Howard, his brother, should be admitted of your College, and desiring that they may see this Commencement hath written to you to that effect himself, as by the enclosed his Lord's letter you may understand. And both further willed me to send you a particular of his company. His Lord's desire is that for the time they stay in Cambridge, which will be until some few days after the Commencement, they may live a scholastic life, and lodge in the College, if it may conveniently be done; with such their company as must of necessity be near them as by inclosed note you may perceive. The rest of their followers, if there be no room in the College shall be provided for in the town, as near your college as possibly may be. In this his Lord assures himself of your best and friendly furtherance and will acknowledge your courtesy as shall be offered. The time of their arrival in Cambridge will be (God willing) on Monday or Tuesday next at the furthest. And so with my best respects unto you I rest

To be commanded by you
John Borough

London 25 June, 1624.

A Note of my Lord Maltravers' Company

My Lord Maltravers and his brother Mr. William Howard to be Lodged in one Chamber of the College, with a pallet for the grooms of their chamber for which there is stuff sent from hence to furnish it, and another outward chamber.

A chamber in the College for my Lord Sandys and his man.

A chamber in the College for Sir Henry Bourchier and his man.

In all five chambers to be provided in the College if it may be.

The rest of his Lordship's company being two gentlemen, a groom of his stable and a footman may be lodged in the town near the College.

To my very assured friend Mr. Doctor Gwinne, Master of St. John's College in Cambridge.

Good Mr. Doctor Gwinne, my son being desirous to spend some few days now at Cambridge, and make himself a member of that famous University, where many of my family have been. I could not deny his suit, as although I am desirous he should be of St. John's your College, where my father and uncles were scholars. I pray make it no trouble in the world unto you, for both I and my son himself desire he may for this beginning live as much as may be according to the rule of a scholar to give him a good entrance that, what he wants now in staying long time he may supply in regularity. So very hearty commendations I rest your assured friend

Arundel and Surrey

Arundel House
25 June 1624

I have entreated my good friend Mr. Borough that he will write unto you of the particulars of my son's company.

8

KING CHARLES I SAYS FAREWELL

1649

Charles I, like his father, James I, was a fervent believer in the divine right of kings. He resented the power of Parliament and aroused the bitter antagonism of its Puritan majority. Civil war broke out and Charles, after an unfair trial, was sentenced to be beheaded.

After taking an affectionate and impressively controlled leave of his children and his political followers, he went to his execution with dignity and courage. On a day of intense cold the king walked calmly to the black-draped scaffold guarded by armed men, both mounted and on foot, for many of the common people were ardent royalists. Against the soldiers pressed a vast, silent throng of men and women to whom the king addressed a final speech of farewell.

Charles I then placed his head on the block and, a king to the last, gave the signal for the executioner to do his work.

Philip Henry, a witness to the tragic scene, wrote in his diary: "At the instant whereof, I remember well, there was such a grone by the thousands then present as I never heard before and desire I may never hear again."

HIS MAJESTY CHARLES I
SAYS FAREWELL TO HIS COMMISSIONERS

My Lords,

You are come to take your leave of me, and I believe we shall scarce ever see each other again—but God's will be done. I thank God I have made my peace with Him, and shall without fear undergo what He shall please men to do to me.

My Lords, you cannot but know that in my fall and ruin you see your own, and that also near to you. I pray God send you better friends than I have found.

I am fully informed of the whole carriage of the plot against me and mine, and nothing so much afflicts me as the sense and feelings I have of the sufferings of my subjects, and the mischief that hangs over my three Kingdoms, drawn upon them by those who (upon pretences of good) violently pursue their own interests and ends.

These words His Majesty delivered with much alacrity and cheerfulness, with a serene countenance, and carriage free from all disturbance.

Thus he parted with the Lords leaving many tender impressions (if not in them) yet in the other hearers.

Brave King Charles I talks quietly to his children before going to his death.

CHARLES I

by

Andrew Marvell

1621–1678

He nothing common did or mean
Upon that memorable scene,
  But with his keener eye
  The axe's edge did try;
Nor called the god, with vulgar spite,
To vindicate his helpless right;
  But bowed his comely head
  Down, as upon a bed.

Gossip of the Seventeenth & Eighteenth Centuries

by John Beresford

KING CHARLES I's LAST WORDS TO HIS CHILDREN — ELIZABETH, AGE 13, AND THE DUKE OF GLOUCESTER, AGE 8.

Monday, 30th January 1649.

His children being come to meet him, he first gave his blessing to the Lady Elizabeth, and bad her remember to tell her brother James, when ever she should see him, that it was his father's last desire, that he should no more look upon Charles as his eldest brother only, but be obedient unto him as his Sovereign; and that they should love one another, and forgive their father's enemies.

Then said the King to her, "Sweetheart, you'll forget this." "No," said she, "I shall never forget it while I live," and pouring forth abundance of tears promised him to write down the particulars.

Then the King, taking the Duke of Gloucester upon his knee said, "Sweetheart, now they will cut off thy father's head." (Upon which words the child looked very stedfastly at him.) "Mark, child, what I say. They will cut off my head, and perhaps make thee a King; but mark what I say, you must not be a King, so long as your brothers Charles and James do live. For they will cut off your brothers' heads when they can catch them, and cut off thy head too at the last; and therefore I charge you, do not be made a King by them."

At which the child, sighing, said, "I will be torn in pieces first." Which, falling so unexpectedly from one so young, it made the King rejoice exceedingly.

9

AN AGREEMENT IS SIGNED AT CAMBRIDGE

1629

The leader of the second wave of migration that left England for America in 1630 was John Winthrop, a future governor of Massachusetts. An attorney by profession, Winthrop was a member of a family of landed gentry. He collected around him a group of wealthy men—the first of this caliber to go to the American colonies. All of them were discouraged with conditions in England and were fearful of approaching calamities.

The following excerpt is taken from the agreement drawn up by these men at Cambridge, England, August 26, 1629. This was the first step toward self-government, entirely independent of a London sponsor, and it foreshadowed that impatience with foreign control which a century later resulted in the severance of all ties with the mother country.

AUGUST 26, 1629

Upon due consideration of the state of the Plantation now in hand for New England, wherein we, whose names are hereunto subscribed, have engaged ourselves, and having weighed the greatness of the work in regard of the consequences, God's glory and the Church's good; as also in regard of the difficulties and discouragements which in all probabilities must be forecast upon the prosecution of this business: considering withal that this whole adventure grows upon the joint confidence we have in each other's fidelity and resolution herein, so as no man of us would have adventured it without assurance of the rest; now, for the better encouragement of ourselves and others that shall join us in this action, and to the end that every man may without scruple dispose of his estate and affairs as may best fit his preparation for this voyage, it is fully and faithfully agreed amongst us, and everyone of us doth hereby freely and sincerely promise and bind himself . . . that we will so really endeavour the prosecution of this work, as by God's assistance, we will be ready in our persons, and with such of our several families as are to go with us . . . to embark for the said Plantation by the first of March next, at such port or ports of this land as shall be agreed upon by the Company, to the end to pass the Seas, (under God's protection) to inhabit and continue in New England; Provided always that, before the last of September next, the whole Government, together with the patent for the said Plantation, be first, by an order of Court, legally transferred and established to remain with us and others which shall inhabit upon the said Plantation; and provided, also, that if any shall be hindered by such just and inevitable let or other cause, to be allowed by three parts of four of those whose names are hereunto subscribed, then such persons, for such times and during such lets, to be discharged of this Bond. And we do further promise, every one for himself, that shall fail to be ready through his own default by the day appointed, to pay for every day's default the sum of three pounds, to the use of the rest of the company who shall be ready by the same day and tide.

Signed:

Richard Saltonstall	Isaac Johnson	John Winthrop
Thomas Dudley	John Humfrey	William Pinchon
William Vassall	Thomas Sharpe	Kellam Browne
Nicholas West	Increase Nowell	William Colbron

10

THE CLERGY SUFFERS AND A CATHEDRAL DEVASTATED

1643

In the wake of the long struggle between Charles I and his Parliament, the Established Church was caught between the warring factions. A small Puritan majority pushed through the Root and Branch Bill, which abolished the episcopacy, and the Grand Remonstrance, which demanded a parliamentary reformation of the church. It was the beginning of the civil war that culminated in the beheading of Charles I.

The magnificent Cathedral of Norwich was situated in the eastern part of the country, which was predominantly Parliamentarian and Puritan—a hotbed of anticlericalism. Dr. Sterne's account of his imprisonment and Bishop Hall's description of the sacking of his cathedral are typical examples of the rough treatment suffered by the Established Church in the tug-of-war between king and parliament.

THE SUFFERINGS OF THE CLERGY

by Dr. Richard Sterne, master of Jesus College, Cambridge
[Afterward Archbishop of York]

Ely House Prison, Oct. 9, 1643

This is now the fourteenth month of my imprisonment: nineteen weeks in the Tower, thirty weeks in the Lord Petre's house, ten days in the ships, and seven weeks in Ely House. The very fees and rents of these several prisons have amounted to above £100, beside[s] diet and all other charges, which have been various and excessive as in prisons is usual. For the better enabling me to maintain myself in prison and my family at home, they have seized upon all my means which they can lay their hands on. And all this while I have never been so much as spoken withal, or called either to give or receive an account why I am here, Nor is anything laid to my charge (not so much as the general crime of my being a malignant), no, not in the warrant for my commitment. What hath been wanting in human justice, hath been, I praise God, supplied by Divine mercy. Health of body, and patience, and cheerfulness of mind, I have not wanted, no, not on shipboard, where we lay, the first night without anything under or over us but the bare decks and the clothes on our backs; and after we had some of us got beds, were not able, when it rained, to lie dry in them, and when it was fair weather, were sweltered with heat, and stifled with our own breaths, there being of us in that one small Ipswich coal-ship (so low-built, too, that we could not walk or stand upright in it) within one or two of three score; whereof six knights, and eight doctors in divinity, and divers gentlemen of very good worth, that would have been sorry to have seen their servants, nay, their dogs, no better accommodated. Yet among all that company, I do not remember that I saw one sad or dejected countenance all the while; so strong is God, when we are weakest.

THE DEVASTATION OF THE CATHEDRAL AT NORWICH

by Bishop Hall

The Sheriff Toftes and Alderman Lindsay, attended with many zealous followers, came into my chapel to look for superstitious pictures and relics of idolatry, and sent for me to let me know they found those windows full of images, which were very offensive, and must be demolished. I told them they were the pictures of some famous and worthy bishops, as St. Ambrose, Austin, etc. It was answered me, that they were popes; and one younger man among the rest would take upon him to defend that every diocesian bishop was pope. I answered him with some scorn, and obtained leave that I might, with the least loss and defacing of the windows, give order for taking off that offence, which I did by causing the heads of those pictures to be taken off, since I knew the bodies could not offend. There was not care and moderation used in reforming the cathedral church bordering upon my palace. It is no other than tragical to relate the carriage of that furious sacrilege, whereof our eyes and ears were the sad witnesses. . . . Lord, what work was here, what clattering of glass, what beating down of walls, what tearing up of monuments, what pulling down of seats, what wresting out of irons and brass from the windows and graves, what defacing of arms, what demolishing of curious stone-work, that had not any representation in the world; but only the cost of the founder and the skill of the mason; what tooting and piping upon the destroyed organ-pipes; and what a hideous triumph on the market-day before all the country, when in a kind of sacrilegious and profane procession, all the organ-pipes, vestments, both copes and surplices, together with the leaden cross, which had been newly sawn down from over the Greenyard pulpit, and the service books and singing books that could be had, were carried to the fire in the public market-place; a lewd wretch walking before the train, in his cope trailing in the dirt, with a service-book in his hand, imitating in an impious scorn, the tune, and usurping the rods of the litany used formerly in the church. Near the public cross all these instruments of idolatry must be sacrificed to the fire, not without much ostentation of a zealous joy in discharging obedience, to the cost of some who professed how much they had longed to see that day. Neither was it any news, upon the guild day, to have the cathedral, now open on all sides, to be filled with musketeers, waiting for the mayor's return, drinking and tobaccoing as freely as if it had turned alehouse.

11

INDICTMENTS FOR WITCHCRAFT

c. 1645

Between 1541 and 1644 executions of eighty witches were recorded in five English counties. During that same period, 513 persons were accused and 790 indictments were filed. These unfortunate women were tortured in order to force confessions from them.

In America much has been told about the witch-hunts of Salem, Massachusetts, in 1692. During this period of mass hysteria, 150 people were imprisoned, 50 were brainwashed into "confessions," 20 were put to death and many others were awaiting trial when —the final absurdity—the president of Harvard College and other prominent citizens were accused. At this point the authorities took fright and stopped the trials.

Witch-hunting was an example of one of the less desirable inheritances from the mother country.

MOTHER SHIPTON'S PROPHECIES
Seventeenth Century

Carriages without horses shall go,
And accidents fill the world with woe.

Around the world thoughts shall fly
In the twinkling of an eye

Under water men shall walk,
Shall ride, shall sleep, shall talk;

In the air men shall be seen
In white, in black, and in green.

INDICTMENTS FOR WITCHCRAFT

Depositions [Seventeenth Century]

ELIZABETH GREENE DE WINCKFIELD

Jo Browneinge testifies that she confessed the day after her apprehending that she was a witch and he asked her how she knew it and she answered she knew it by the tokens found about her. He asking her how these tokens came, she said that Goody Wright of Stradbrooke sent her 3 imps which she found at home like 3 chickens. She called these imps Giles Alse and Bes and further the devil appeared to her like a man one night when she was in bed asleep and nipped her by the neck and wakened her and that he took her by the hand and asked her if she would serve him, but she did not confess that she did assent, but said he drew 3 drops of blood of her arm and showed the place where he drew it and that he asked her to keep some imps which she told him she would and after, she suckled her 3 imps. She refused the money the devil offered her.

ELIZABETH RICHMOND DE BRAMFORD

After six days watching she confessed that the devil came to her and embraced her and asked her to love him and trust in him and he would defend her and curse her enemies and she asked him who he was and he said the prophet Daniel and he told her she must forsake God and the Church and that she must not go to Church which she promised upon her troth she would do. And after this, being angry with one Goody Furnis she wished the plague on her and she died within six weeks and as she thought it was upon her cursing.

JOHN CHAMBERS

[When he was] *about twelve years the Devil told him in the shape of a boy that if he would follow his directions and make a covenant with him he should want for nothing and that he brought a writing to him and he drew blood of his finger and signed the covenant and the devil promised to find him 3 imps which accordingly he received, and employed these imps to kill a bullock of Widman's and an horse of another man's and he sent his imp Richard to kill one Smith's horse and it died, and he sent his imp John to kill one Smith's child and it died.*

Smith testified that Chambers confessed freely that he was the cause that sent two toads to his wife as she was dressing her child and that he came back to his house to see if the toads had done what he sent them for and that the child which she was then dressing did forthwith languish and die.

LIDEA TAYLOR, WIFE

John Beomeny testifies that she was apprehended the 30th of July and about the ____ day of August she confessed that she was a witch & that she had 2 imps the one like an owl, the other like a blackbird and that by these means she killed one Bert's cattle and that he and all his house were the worse for her and that her imps counselled her to steal and that they counselled her to kill herself, and that the devil did appear to her in the night but she called her husband.

MILLS, WIFE OF DE FFRESINGFIELD

Jna Goodinge testifies that after two nights watching she confessed she had 3 birds some call them imps. Their names are Tom, Robert and John and that she gave one of those birds to one of Tho. Aldus' children which broke out with 21 sores and died; that she sent 2 of her birds to 2 of Page's children and both of them likewise had sores and one of them died and that she sent one of her birds to Goodman's locks which caused one of his cows to skip over a stile and burst her neck which happened accordingly and that Tom caused John Wolnose's horse to throw him in the water, & Robert caused Aldus's cart to stand fast on the plain ground, and that the devil drew blood of her and wrote with it but what he wrote she knew not.

SUSANNA SMITH DE RUSHMERE, WIFE

Robert Mayhew testified that the next day after her apprehension she confessed that 18 years since the devil appeared to her like a red, shaggy dog and tempted her to kill her children but she strove with him 24 hours before he went from her but she would not kill them. But being desired to relate further of her witchcraft there rose two swellings in her throat so that she could not speak, but he came to her the next night and she confessed that the devil did again appear to her in the likeness of a black bee and told her that she should be attached the next day and that if she confessed anything, she should die for it and being demanded why she would eat nothing there being good meat provided for her, she said the devil told her she should never eat nor drink again but they then brought her meat and with much trembling she got some down and further said that the devil came to her and that she would not confess until he went from her again. But after he was gone she confessed that she had signed a covenant with the devil at his first appearance and signed it with a cross and after that the devil wrote her name to that covenant to which she had made that mark and that the devil had told her where there was a rusty knife in the room wherewith she might kill herself and they looked in that place & found such an old knife as she described but she said that she could not kill herself because they were in the room.

12

AFTER CROMWELL, CHARLES II

1658–1659

John Evelyn, author, linguist, royalist, and friend of Samuel Pepys, was one of the most renowned and respected diarists of his time. He knew personally both King Charles II and King James II, and he was on intimate terms with the ministers of those two monarchs, acting as confidant to many of the eminent men of his day.

An observer of the funeral of Cromwell, as well as one of the onlookers at the jubilant return from exile of Charles II, his eyewitness descriptions of both events are moving in their simple and vivid pictures of those turbulent times.

FUNERAL OF CROMWELL AND RETURN OF CHARLES II

by Sir John Evelyn

Oct. 22nd. 1658. Saw the superb funeral of the Protector. He was carried from Somerset-House in a velvet bed of state, drawn by six horses, housed with the same; the pall held by his new

Lords; Oliver lying in effigy, in royal robes, and crowned with a crown, sceptre, and globe, like a king. The pendants and guidons were carried by the officers of the army; the imperial banners, achievements, etc. by the heralds in their coats; a rich caparisoned horse, embroidered all over with gold; a knight of honour, armed cap-a-pie, and, after all, his guards, soldiers, and innumerable mourners. In this equipage, they proceeded to Westminster: but it was the joyfullest funeral I ever saw; for there were none that cried but dogs, which the soldiers hooted away with a barbarous noise, drinking and taking tobacco in the streets as they went.

April 25th. 1659. A wonderful and sudden change in the face of the public; the new Protector, Richard, slighted; several pretenders and parties strive for the government: all anarchy and confusion; Lord have mercy on us!

February 3d. 1660. General Monk came now to London out of Scotland; but no man knew what he would do, or declare, yet he was met on his way by the gentlemen of all the counties which he passed, with petitions that he would recall the old long interrupted Parliament, and settle the nation in some order, being at this time in most prodigious confusion, and under no government, everybody expecting what would be next, and what he would do.

February 10th. Now were the gates of the city broken down by General Monk; which exceedingly exasperated the city, the soldiers marching up and down as triumphing over it, and all the old army of the fanatics . . . sent out of town.

February 11th. A signal day. Monk, perceiving how infamous and wretched a pack of knaves would have still usurped the supreme power, and having intelligence that they intended to take away his commission, repenting of what he had done to the city, and where he and his forces were quartered, marches to Whitehall, dissipates that nest of robbers, and convenes the old Parliament, the Rump Parliament (so called as retaining some few rotten members of the other) being dissolved; and for joy whereof were many thousands of rumps roasted publicly in the streets at the bonfires this night, with ringing of bells, and universal jubilee. This was the first good omen.

May 3d. Came the most happy tidings of his Majesty's gracious declaration and applications to the Parliament, General, and People, and their most dutiful acceptance and acknowledgement, after a most bloody and unreasonable rebellion of near twenty years. Praised be for ever the Lord of Heaven, who only doeth wondrous things, because His mercy endureth for ever!

May 29th. This day, his Majesty Charles the Second came to London, after a sad and long exile and calamitous sufferings both of the King and Church, being seventeen years. This was also his birth-day, and with a triumph of above 20,000 horse and foot, brandishing their swords, and shouting, with inexpressible joy; the ways strewed with flowers, the bells ringing, the streets hung with tapestries, fountains running with wine; the Mayor, Aldermen, and all the Companies, in their liveries, chains of gold, and banners; Lords and Nobles everybody clad in cloth of silver, gold, and velvet; the windows and balconies, all set with ladies; trumpets, music, and myriads of people flocking the streets, even so far as from Rochester, so as they were seven hours in passing the city, even from two in the afternoon until nine at night.

I stood in the Strand and beheld it, and blessed God. And all this was done without one drop of blood shed, and by that very army which rebelled against him; but it was the Lord's doing, for such a restoration was never mentioned in any history, ancient or modern, since the return of the Jews from the Babylonish captivity; nor so joyful a day and so bright ever seen in this nation, this happening when to expect or effect it was past all human policy.

1661. 30th January. Was the first solemn fast and day of humiliation to deplore the sins which so long had provoked God against this afflicted church and people, ordered by Parliament to be annually celebrated to expiate the guilt of the execrable murder of the late King.

This day (O the stupendous and inscrutable judgments of God!) were the carcasses of those arch-rebels, Cromwell, Bradshawe, (the judge who condemned his Majesty), and Ireton (son-in-law to the Usurper), dragged out of their superb tombs in Westminster among the Kings, to Tyburn, and hanged on the gallows there from nine in the morning till six at night, and then buried under the fatal and ignominious monument in a deep pit; thousands of people who had seen them in all their pride being spectators.

13

OUTBREAK OF THE PLAGUE IN LONDON

1665

In 1665 the bubonic plague raged throughout England. All through the Middle Ages there had been outbreaks of this deadly disease which was carried by rats and encouraged by a total lack of what today we call sanitation. In the summer of 1665 the death toll from this ghastly sickness reached an all-time high. Men, women, and children—possibly 170,000 of them—died in London alone in the space of a few months. Everyone who could fled to the country.

Samuel Pepys, Secretary of the Admiralty, sent his family away, but, detained by official duties, he himself remained in the capital for the greater part of the summer. Pepys' description of the plague-stricken city is a classic of eyewitness reporting. His personal accounts of contemporary events have made Pepys one of the best-known diarists of all time.

OUTBREAK OF THE PLAGUE IN LONDON

by Samuel Pepys

April 30, 1665: Great fears of the sicknesse here in the City, it being said that two or three houses are already shut up. God preserve us all!

May 7, 1665: This day, much against my will, I did in Drury Lane see two or three houses marked with a red cross upon the doors, and "Lord have mercy upon us" writ there; which was a sad sight to me, being the first of the kind that, to my remembrance, I ever saw. It put me into an ill conception of myself and my smell, so that I was forced to buy some roll-tobacco to smell to and chaw, which took away the apprehension.

May 10, 1665: In the evening home, and there to my great trouble hear that the plague is come into the City: but where should it begin but in my good friend and neighbour's, Dr. Burnett, in Fenchurch Street, which in both points troubles me mightily.

May 15, 1665: The towne grows very sickly, and people to be afeard of it, there dying this last week of the plague 112 from 43 the week before. It struck me very deep this afternoon going with a hackney coach from my Lord Treasurer's down Holborne, the coachman I found to drive easily and easily, at last stood still, and come down hardly able to stand, and told me that he was suddenly struck very sicke, and almost blind, he could not see. So I 'light and went into another coach with a sad heart for the poor man and trouble for myself lest he should have been struck with the plague, being at the end of the towne that I took him up: but God have mercy upon us all!

May 21, 1665: To the Cross Keys at Cripplegate, where I find all the towne almost going out of towne, the coaches and waggons being full of people going into the country.

May 22: In great pain whether to send my mother into the country today or no. At last I resolved to put it to her, and she agreed to go, so I would not oppose it, because of the sicknesse in the towne, and my intentions of removing my wife.

May 29: This end of the towne every day grows very bad of the plague.

June 13: Above 700 died of the plague this week.
June 30: It was a sad noise to hear our bell to toll and ring so often today, either for deaths or burials: I think five or six times.
August 9: The streets mighty empty all the way now even in London; which is a sad sight. And to Westminster Hall, where talking, hearing very sad stories. Poor Will, that used to sell us ale at the Hall-door, his wife and three children died, all I think in one day. So home through the City again, wishing I may have taken no ill in going, but I will go I think, no more thither.
August 12: The people die so that now it seems they are fain to carry the dead to be buried by day-light, the nights not sufficing to do it in. And my Lord Mayor commands people to be within at nine at night, all as they say that the sick may have liberty to go abroad for ayre.
August 15: By water to the Duke of Albermarle with whom I spoke a great deale in private. It was dark before I could get home, and so land at Churchyard stairs, where to my great trouble, I met a dead corpse of the plague in the narrow ally just bringing down a little pair of stairs. But I thank God I was not much disturbed at it. However, I shall beware of being late abroad again.
August 31: Up: and after putting several things in order to my removal, to Woolwich. Thus this month ends with great sadness upon the publick, through the greatness of the plague every where through the kingdom almost. In the City died this week 7,496, and of them 6,102 of the plague. But it is feared that the true number of the dead this week is near 10,000; partly from the poor that cannot be taken notice of through the greatness of the number, and partly from the Quakers and others that will not have any bell ring for them.
September 3: (Lord's Day.) Up and put on my coloured silk suit very fine, and my new periwigg, bought a good while since but durst not wear because the plague was in Westminster when I bought it; and it is a wonder what will be the fashion after the plague is done as to periwiggs, for nobody will dare to buy any haire for fear of the infection that it had been cut off of the heads of people dead of the plague.

I up to the Vestry at the desire of the Justices of the Peace, in order to do something for the keeping of the plague from growing; but, Lord! to consider the madness of the people of the town, who will (because they are forbid) come in crowds alongwith the dead corpse to see them buried: but we agreed on some orders for the prevention thereof.

Among other stories one was very passionate, methought, of a complaint brought against a man in the towne for taking a child from London from an infected house. Alderman Hooker told us it was the child of a very able citizen in Gracious Street, a saddler, who had buried all the rest of his children of the plague, and himself and wife now being shut up and despair of escaping, did desire only to save the life of this little child: and so prevailed to have it received stark-naked into the arms of a friend, who brought it to Greenwich; whereupon hearing the story, we did agree it should be permitted to be received and kept in the towne.

September 6th: Busy all morning writing letters . . . so to dinner, to London; and there I looked into the street and saw fires burning in the street, as it is through the whole City, by the Lord Mayor's order. Thence by water to the Duke of Albermarle's; all the way fires on each side of the Thames; and strange to see in broad daylight two or three burials upon the Banke-side, one at the very heels of another; doubtless all of the plague, and yet at least forty or fifty people going along with every one of them.

September 15: But Lord! what a sad time it is to see no boats upon the river: and grass grows all up and down White Hall court, and nobody but poor wretches in the streets!

September 30: Great joy we have this week in the weekly Bill, it being come to 544 in all, and but 333 of the plague, so that we are encouraged to get to London soon as we can.

December 31: But now the plague is abating almost to nothing and I intending to get to London as fast as I can. . . . But many of such as I know very well, dead: yet to our great joy the town fills apace, and shops begin to be open again. Pray God continue the plague's decrease!

14

THE FIRE OF LONDON

1666

As the bubonic plague was slowly abating, London reeled under another disaster—the Great Fire.

No one knows how or even where the conflagration started. But by three o'clock in the morning of September 2, 1666, the flames were out of control and raging through the small wooden houses at both ends of London Bridge.

Samuel Pepys was once more not only the historian of this drama but one of its actors. Setting off on an inspection tour of the city, he soon saw that a major disaster was in the making. Fanned by a high wind and abetted by the long drought that had dried out the wood of the ancient houses so that they were as inflammable as tinder, the fire seemed likely to make London a disaster area.

Pepys rushed off to Whitehall Palace, where he was received by the king. Then he raced back to find the lord mayor who, according to the diarist, was "behaving like a fainting woman." Man of action as well as detached observer, Pepys, the indefatigable diarist, gives an unforgettable picture of the doomed city. As a result of its trial by fire, London had to be almost completely rebuilt.

THE GREAT FIRE

by Samuel Pepys

Some of our maids, sitting up late last night to get things ready against our feast today, Jane called us up about three in the morning to tell us of a great fire they saw in the City. So I rose and slipped on my nightgown, and went to her window, and thought it to be on the back side of Mark Lane at the farthest; but, being unused to such fires as followed, I thought it far enough off; and so went to bed again and to sleep.

About seven rose again to dress myself, and there looked out at the window and saw the fire not so much as it was, and further off. By and by Jane comes and tells me that she hears that about 300 houses have been burned down tonight by the fire we saw, and that it is now burning down Fish Street, by London Bridge.

So I made myself ready presently, and walked to the Tower, and there got up upon one of the high places; and there I did see the houses at that end of the bridge all on fire, and an infinite great fire on this and the other side the end of the bridge. So with my heart full of trouble I down to the waterside, and there got a boat to pass through the bridge, and there saw a lamentable fire.

Poor Mitchell's house, as far as the Old Swan already burned that way and the fire running further. Everybody endeavoring to remove their goods, and flinging into the river or bringing them into lighters that lay off; poor people staying in their houses as long as till the very fire touched them, and then running into boats, or clambering from one pair of stairs by the waterside to another. And among other things the poor pigeons, I perceive, were loth to leave their houses, but hovered about the windows and balconys till they were, some of them, burned their wings, and fell down.

Having staid, and in an hour's time, seen the fire rage every way, and nobody, to my sight, endeavoring to quench it, but to remove their goods and leave all to the fire; and having seen it get as far as the Steel Yard, and the wind mighty high, and driving it into the City, and everything after so long a drought proving combustible, even the very stones of churches, I to Whitehall, and there up to the King's closet in the Chapel, where people come about me, and I did give them an account dismayed them all, and word was carried in to the King.

So I was called for, and did tell the King and Duke of York what I saw, and that unless His Majesty did command houses to be pulled down nothing could stop the fire.

They seemed much troubled, and the King commanded me to go to my Lord Mayor from him and command him to spare no houses, but to pull down before the fire every way. The Duke of York bid me tell him that if he would have any more soldiers he shall. Here meeting with Captain Cooke, I in his coach which he lent me, and Creed with me to Paul's, and there walked along Watling St. as well as I could, every creature coming away laden with goods to save, and here and there sick people carried away in beds. Extraordinary good goods carried in carts and on backs.

At last met my Lord Mayor in Canning St. like a man spent, with a handkerchief about his neck. To the King's message, he cried like a fainting woman, "Lord, what can I do? I am spent; people will not obey me. I have been pulling down houses, but the fire overtakes us faster than we can do it." That he needed no more soldiers; and that, for himself, he must go and refresh himself, having been up all night. So he left me, and I him, and walked home, seeing people all almost distracted, and no manner of means used to quench the fire.

Having seen as much as I could now, I away to Whitehall by appointment, and there walked to St. James Park, and there met my wife and Creed, and walked to my boat; and there upon the water again, and to the fire up and down, it still increasing, and the wind great. So near the fire as we could for smoke; and all over the Thames, with one's face in the wind, you were almost burned with a shower of fire drops.

When we could endure no more upon the water, we to a little ale-house on the Bankside, over against the Three Cranes, and there staid till it was dark almost, and saw the fire grow; and, as it grew darker, appeared more and more in corners and upon steeples, and between churches and houses, as far as we could see up the hill of the City, in a most horrid, malicious, bloody flame, not like the fine flame of an ordinary fire. We staid still, it being darkish, we saw the fire as only one entire arch of fire from this to the other side of the bridge, and in a bow up the hill for an arch of above a mile long. It made me weep to see it. The churches, houses and all on fire and flaming at once, and a horrid noise the flames made, and the cracking of houses at their ruin. So home with a sad heart, and there find poor Tom Hater come with some few of his goods saved out of the house, which is burned.

I invited him to lie at my house, and did receive his goods, but was deceived, the news coming every moment of the growth of the fire. So we were forced to begin to pack up our own goods, and prepare for their removal. And did by moonshine carry much of my goods into the garden, and Mr. Hater and I did remove my money and iron chests into my cellar, as thinking that the safest place. And got my bags of gold into my office ready to carry away, and my chief papers of accounts also there, and my tallys into a box by themselves.

About four in the morning my Lady Batten sent me a cart to carry away all my money and plate and best things to Sir W. Rider's at Bednall Green; which I did, riding myself in my night-gown in the cart. Lord! to see how the streets and the highways are crowded with people running and riding, and getting of carts at any rate to fetch away things. I find Sir W. Rider tired with being called up all night, and receiving things from several friends. I am eased at my heart to have my treasure. . . .

I after dark walked to Tower Street, and there saw it all on fire. Now begins the practice of blowing up of houses in Tower Street, those next the Tower, which at first did frighten people more than anything. All the Old Bailey and Paul's is burned, and all Cheapside.

Home and whereas I expected to have seen our house on fire it was not. For my confidence of finding our Office on fire was such that I durst not ask anybody how it was with us till I come and saw it not burned.

Walked into Moorefields (our feet ready to burn, walking through the town among the hot coals). Drank there and paid two pence for a plain penny loaf. I also did see a poor cat taken out of a hole in the chimney, joining to the wall of the Exchange, with the hair all burned off the body, but still alive.

So home at night. Lay down and slept a good night about midnight.

This drawing shows St. Peter's Church on Eaton Square, Pimlico. Like many handsome churches built after the Great Fire of London, it is typical of Sir Christopher Wren's style of architecture.

15

JOHN BUNYAN,

THE PILGRIM'S PROGRESS

1678

The first edition of The Pilgrim's Progress *appeared in 1678. Famous as soon as it was published, the work is universally recognized as one of the masterpieces of the English language.*

Its author, John Bunyan, was born in the tiny village of Elstow, one mile from the county town of Bedford. His father was a brazier. As a boy Bunyan learned to read and write—an unusual accomplishment for those days. When he was in his teens the civil war broke out and for the next three years Bunyan served as a soldier in the Parliamentary army. After his marriage some five years later, Bunyan developed an interest in religion, joined the Puritan community in Bedford, and became a preacher.

With the Restoration, Puritan preachers were not permitted to preach. Bunyan was now a leader of the Puritan community.

Defying the law, he addressed a meeting in November, 1660, was arrested and thrown into prison, where he remained for the next twelve years. He occupied his time in jail by writing at least twenty religious books in prose and verse.

The Pilgrim's Progress *is an allegory. It tells the story of man's life as a pilgrimage, the pilgrimage of John Bunyan himself. Written in plain English, it is as readable today as it was then.*

THE PILGRIM'S PROGRESS

by John Bunyan

Now as they were going along and talking they espied a boy feeding his father's sheep. The boy was in very mean clothes, but of a very fresh and well-favoured countenance, and as he sat by himself, he sang. "Hark," saith Mr. Greatheart, "to what the shepherd boy saith." So they hearkened, and he said:

He that is down needs fear no fall,
He that is low, no pride:
He that is humble ever shall
Have God to be his guide.

I am content with what I have,
Little be it or much;
And, Lord, contentment still I crave,
Because thou savest such.

Fulness to such a burden is
That go on pilgrimage:
Here little, and hereafter bliss,
Is best from age to age.

Then said their guide, "Do you hear him? I will dare to say that this boy lives a merrier life, and wears more of that herb called heartsease in his bosom, than he that is clad in silk and velvet: but we will proceed in our discourse."

"In this valley our Lord formerly had his country house; he loved much to be here; he loved also to walk these meadows, for he found the air was pleasant. Besides, here a man shall be free from the noise and the hurryings of this life. All states are full of noise and confusion, only the Valley of Humiliation is that empty and solitary place. Here a man shall not be so let and hindered in his contemplation as in other places he is apt to be. This is a Valley that nobody walks in but those that love a Pilgrim's life. . . ."

After this it was noised abroad that Mr. Valiant-for-Truth was taken with a summons by the same post as the other, and had this for a token that the summons was true, that his pitcher was broken at the fountain. When he understood it, he called for his friends, and told them of it. Then said he, I am going to my Father's, and though with great difficulty I am got hither, yet now I do not repent me of all the trouble I have been at to arrive where I am. My sword I give to him that shall succeed me in my pilgrimage, and my courage and skill to him that can get it. My marks and scars I carry with me, to be a witness for me that I have fought his battles who now will be my rewarder. When the day that he must go hence was come, many accompanied him to the riverside, into which, as he went, he said "Death, where is thy sting?"

And as he went down deeper he said, "Grave, where is thy victory?"

So he passed over, and all the trumpets sounded for him on the other side.

16

THE AMUSEMENTS OF LONDON

1669

On the first of March, 1669, Cosmo the Third, Grand Duke of Tuscany, made a trip to England. This was a tourist jaunt de luxe, and although Cosmo III was received by the king at Hampton Court Palace and in London, he was very much interested in the life of the English people. Whenever he could slip away from ceremonial visits he attended cockfights, deer hunts, public dancing classes, and gladiatorial contests.

Count Lorenzo Magalotti, a learned man and one of the eminent characters of his day, traveled with the Grand Duke, acting as historian of the journey. The account that follows is taken from his memoirs, and gives a picture of English sporting life in the reign of King Charles II.

TRAVELS OF COSMO THE THIRD THROUGH ENGLAND

by Lorenzo Magalotti

His highness went out in his carriage to see the theatre appropriated to cock-fighting, a common amusement of the English, who even in the public streets take a delight in seeing such battles; and their partiality towards these animals is carried to such an height, that considerable bets are made on the victory of the one or the other. To render the cocks fit for fighting, they select the best of the breed, cut off their crest and spurs, keeping them in separate coops or walks, and mix with their usual food pepper, cloves, and other aromatics, and the yolks of eggs, to heat them, and render them more vigorous in battle; and when they want to bring them to the trial, they convey them in a bag, put on artificial spurs, of silver or steel, very long and sharp, and let them out at the place appointed for the sport. As soon as the cocks are put down, they walk round the field of battle with great animation, each waiting for an opportunity to attack his rival with advantage. The first who is attacked places himself in a posture of defence, now spreading himself out, now falling in his turn, on the assailant; and in the progress of the contest, they are inflamed to such a pitch of rage, that it is almost incredible to such as have never witnessed it with what fury each annoys his adversary, striking one another on the head with their beaks, and tearing one another with the spurs, till at length he that feels himself superior, and confident of victory, mounts on the back of his opponent, and never quits him, till he has left him dead, and then, by a natural instinct, crows in applause of his own victory.

The whole of the morning of the twenty-third, he [Cosmo III] passed at home, and went out after dinner in his carriage to one of the principal dancing schools of the metropolis, frequented both by unmarried and married ladies, who are instructed by the master, and practise, with much gracefulness and agility, various dances after the English fashion. Dancing is a very common and favorite amusement of the ladies in this country; every evening there are entertainments at different places in the city, at which many ladies and citizens' wives are present, they going to them alone, as they do to the rooms of the dancing masters, at which there are frequently upwards of forty or fifty ladies. His highness had an opportunity of seeing several dances in the English style, exceedingly well regulated, and executed in the smartest and genteelest manner by very young ladies, whose beauty and gracefulness were shewn off to perfection by this exercise. This is a sufficient proof of the liberty enjoyed by the ladies in London, who are not prohibited from walking in the streets by night as well as by day, without any attendance. By day they go on foot or in their carriages, either *incog.* with masks or without, as they think proper; because it is not the custom to salute them more than once, not even in the Mall, or Hyde Park, although they are acquaintances; and they would be offended by a repetition of the salutation.

Having spent some time in this amusement, his highness went to see an hydraulic machine, raised upon a wooden tower, in the neighborhood of Somerset House, which is used for conveying the water of the river to the greater part of the city. It is put in motion by two horses, which are continually going round, it not being possible that it should receive its movement from the current of the river, as in many other places where the rivers never vary in their course; but this is not the case with the Thames, owing to the tide; the wheels, which serve at the ebb, would not be able to do their office when the tide returns.

His highness passed the morning of the twenty-fourth in his usual occupations, and in writing, and went out after dinner to see the gladiators, or fencing masters, who, in order to get reputation, give a general challenge, offering twenty or thirty jacobuses, or more, to any one that has a mind to fight with them. No person is admitted into the theatre without first paying at the door, for the benefit of the challenger, who thus, from the number of curious persons who resort to the exhibition, receives much more than he has presented to his antagonist. They enter the lists, armed with a round shield and a sword not sharpened, fighting with the edge, not with the point, and by an understanding between them, they give over as soon as blood is drawn, consequently it rarely happens that they injure one another seriously; it cannot, however, be denied that this sport has something barbarous in it.

On the morning of the 30th, his highness performed his usual devotional exercises at an early hour, that he might be ready for his projected excursion to Hampton Court. He entered his carriage and set out, followed by the gentlemen of his suite, for the above-mentioned royal residence, which is about twelve miles from London, in order to see the deer-hunting in the adjacent park. On first entering the park, he was met by Prince Robert, who was likewise come hither for the diversion of seeing the hunt. After the usual compliments, his highness went forward, Prince Robert remaining in the place appointed for him under the shade of a tree, on a stage a little raised from the ground, which is the same where the king stands to see this amusement. When the huntsmen had stretched out the nets, after the German manner, inclosing with them a considerable space of land, they let the dogs loose upon four deer which were confined there, who, as soon as they saw them, took to flight; but as they had not the power of going which way they pleased, they ran round the nets, endeavouring by various cunning leaps to save themselves from being stopped by the dogs, and continued to run in this manner for some time, to the great diversion of the spectators, till at last the huntsmen, that they might not harass the animals superfluously, drawing a certain cord, opened the nets in one part, which was prepared for that purpose, and left the deer at liberty to escape.

On his return to London after dinner, his highness went down the Thames in a boat, which had been sent for his accommodation. They made the voyage very expeditiously and agreeably, enjoying the beauty of the river, and landing in due time at the palace of Whitehall. He went immediately to the apartments of the queen, to pay his compliments, where the king soon arrived, and gave him a most courteous welcome, manifesting much curiosity to know if the deer-hunt and the palace, with its environs, had given his highness pleasure.

THE COST OF LIVING: 1681

Prices of Provisions Laid Down by the Chancellor of Oxford University.

	s.	d.
A pound of butter, sweet and new, the best in the market		6
Eggs, six for		2
A couple of fat pullets	2	0
A fat pig, the best in the market	2	0
A stone of the best beef at the butcher's, weighing eight pounds avoirdupois	2	0
A quarter of the best veal at the butcher's, by the pound		3
A pound of cotton or watching candles		5
A bushel of the best oats, within every inn	2	8

[AUTHOR'S NOTE: The shilling (column 1 above) is about 1/20 of a £ or $.24 and 3/4 cents. The penny ("d." is the abbreviation of the Latin word *denarius* for pence or penny) appears in the second column. It was about this time that a box at the theatre cost about 5 s., about $1.25 in U.S. money today.]

17

THESE PEOPLE, THE ENGLISH

1688-1697

From 1688 to 1697, Misson de Valbourg, a Frenchman, lived in England. Young, curious, and perceptive, he observed the life around him, comparing it, sometimes favorably, sometimes unfavorably, with the customs of his native France.

Although critical at times of the heavy eating habits of his hosts and scornful of their lack of grace in reciting poetry, he appreciated the sterling qualities of the English character: "I'm satisfied," he says, "that the more strangers are acquainted with the English, the more they will esteem and love them."

THE ENGLISH

by Misson de Valbourg

The inhabitants of this excellent Country are tall, handsome, well-made, fair, active, robust, courageous, thoughtful, devout, Lovers of the Liberal Arts, and as capable of the Sciences as any People in the World. I can't imagine what could occasion the Notion that I have frequently observed in *France,* That the

English were Treacherous. 'Tis strange, that they, of all Nations of the World, should lie under this Scandal; they, whose Generosity cannot so much bear that two Men should fight without an equality of Arms, Offensive and Defensive: He that should venture to use either Cane or Sword against a Man that had nothing to defend himself with but his Hands, would run a Risque of being torn to pieces by the 'Prentices of the Neighborhood, and by the Mob. 'Tis certainly great Injustice to reckon Treachery among the Vices familiar to the *English*. Other Nations also accuse the common People among the *English* of Incivility, because they generally accost one another without putting their Hands to their Hats, and without that Flood of Compliments that usually pour out of the Mouth of the *French, Italians, etc.* But they take the Thing in a wrong Light; every one follows his own Ideas; and the idea of the *English* is, that Civility does not consist wholly of these outward Shows, which very often are hypocritical and deceitful. I am willing to believe that the *English* are subject to certain Faults, as no doubt all Nations are; but every Thing considered, I'm satisfied, by several Years Experience, that the more Strangers are acquainted with the *English*, the more they will esteem and love them.

They make in *England* the best knives and the worst Scissors in the World. Their Penknifes are so large that you can scarce use any Thing but the Points of 'em.

The *English* have a mighty value for their Poetry. If they believe that their Language is the finest in the whole World, tho' spoken nowhere but in their own Island; they have proportionately a much higher Idea of their Verses: They never read or repeat them without the most singular Tone in the World. When they happen in reading to go out of Prose into Verse, you would swear you no longer heard the same Person; His Tone of Voice becomes soft and tender; . . . he dies away with Rapture.

The People of *England* when they meet, never salute one another, otherwise than by giving one another their Hands, and shaking them heartily; they no more dream of pulling off their Hats, than the Women do of pulling off their Headcloths.

Besides the Sports and Diversions common to most other *European* Nations, as Tennis, Billiards, Chess, Tick-tack, Dancing, Plays, etc., the English have some which are particular to them, or at least which they love and use more than any other People. Any Thing that looks like Fighting, is delicious to an *Englishman.* If two little Boys quarrel in the Street, the Passengers stop, make a Ring round them in a Moment, and set them against one another, that they may come to Fisticuffs. When 'tis come to a Fight, each pulls off his Neckcloth and his Wastcoat, and give them to hold to some of the Standers-by; then they begin to brandish their Fists in the Air; the Blows are aimed all at the Face, they kick one another's Shins, they tug one another by the Hair, etc. He that has got the other down, may give him one Blow or two before he rises, but no more; and let the Boy get up ever so often, the other is obliged to box him again as often as he requires it. During the Fight the Ring of By-standers encourage the combatants with great Delight of Heart, and never part them while they fight according to Rules.

The English of all Sects, but particularly Presbyterians, make Profession of being very strict Observers of the Sabbath Day. I believe their Doctrine upon this Head does not differ from ours, but most assuredly our scruples are much less great than theirs. This appears upon a hundred Occasions; but I have observ'd it particularly in the printed Confessions of Persons that are Hang'd; Sabbath-breaking is the Crime the poor Wretches always begin with. If they had killed Mother and Father, they would not mention that Article, till after having professed how often they had broke the Sabbath. One of the good *English* customs on the Sabbath-day, is to feast as nobly as possible, and especially not to forget the Pudding. It is a common Practice, even among People of good Substance, to have a huge piece of Roast-Beef on *Sundays* of which they stuff till they can swallow no more, and eat the rest cold, without any other Victuals, the other six Days of the Week.

Tobacco is very much used in *England.* The very women take it in abundance, particularly in the Western Counties. Is not this

Two rather bad-mannered old men of the eighteenth century sit down to their huge midday meal.

perpetual Use of Tobacco what makes the Generality of *English* Men so taciturn, so thoughtful, and so melancholy?

The *English* eat a great deal at Dinner; they rest a while, and to it again, till they have quite stuffed their Paunch. Their Supper is moderate: Gluttons at Noon, and abstinent at Night. I always heard they were great Flesheaters, and I found it true. I have known several people in *England* that never eat any Bread, and universally they eat very little: They nibble a few Crumbs, while they chew the Meat by whole mouthfulls. Generally speaking, the *English* Tables are not delicately served. There are some Noblemen that have both *French* and *English* Cooks, and these eat much after the *French* Manner: But among the middling Sort of People, they have ten or twelve Sorts of common Meats, which infallibly take their Turns at their Table, and two Dishes are their Dinners; a Pudding, for instance, and a Piece of roast Beef. Ah, what an excellent Thing is an *English Pudding! To come in Pudding-time,* is as much as to say, to come in the most lucky Moment in the World. Give an *English* Man a *Pudding,* and he shall think it a noble Treat in any Part of the World.

18

GEORGE FOX

1624-1691

George Fox made a unique and important contribution to the history of religion. He believed in the "inner light," or direct personal inspiration, and traveled throughout England, Scotland, Ireland, America, and Germany preaching his gentle gospel.

William Penn, the founder of Pennsylvania and himself a Quaker, wrote the following sympathetic appreciation of his friend and leader.

GEORGE FOX

by William Penn

George Fox was born in Leicestershire, about the year 1624. He descended of honest and sufficient parents, who endeavoured to bring him up, as they did the rest of their children, in the way and worship of the nation; especially his mother, who was a woman accomplished above most of her degree in the place where she lived. But from a child he appeared of another frame of mind than the rest of his brethren; being more religious, inward, still, solid, and observing beyond his years, as the answers he would give, and the questions he would put upon occasion, manifested to the astonishment of those that heard him, especially in divine things.

He was brought up in country business; and as he took most delight in sheep, so he was very skilful in them; an employment that very well suited his mind in several respects, both from its innocency and solitude; and was a just figure of his after ministry and service. When he was somewhat above twenty, he left his friends, and visited the most retired and religious people in those parts; and some there were in this nation, who waited for the consolation of Israel night and day; as Zacharias, Anna, and good old Simeon did of old time. To these he was sent, and these he sought out in the neighbouring counties, and among them he sojourned till his more ample ministry came upon him. At this time he taught and was an example of silence, endeavouring to bring them from self-performances to the Light of Christ within them, and encouraging them to wait in patience to feel the power of it to stir in their hearts. Accordingly, several meetings were gathered in those parts; and thus his time was employed for some years.

In 1652, he being in his usual retirement to the Lord upon a very high mountain, in some higher parts of Yorkshire, as I take it, he had a vision of the great work of God in the earth, and of the way he was to go forth to begin it. He saw people as thick as motes in the sun, that should in time be brought home to the Lord; so that there might be but one shepherd and one sheepfold in all the earth. Upon this mountain he was moved of the Lord to sound forth his great and notable day, and from thence went north, as the Lord had shown him; and in every place where he came, he had his particular exercise and service shown to him, so that the Lord was his leader indeed. For it was not in vain that he travelled, God in most places sealing his commission with the convincement of some of all sorts, as well publicans as sober professors of religion. They [Fox and his followers] were frequently drawn forth, especially to visit the public assemblies, to reprove, inform, and exhort them; sometimes in markets, fairs, streets, and by the highway-side, calling people to repentance, and to turn to the Lord with their hearts as well as their mouths; directing them to the Light of Christ within them. They suffered great hardships for this their love and good-will, being often put in the stocks, stoned, beaten, whipped, and imprisoned. And though the priests generally set themselves to oppose them, and write against them, and insinuated most false and scandalous stories to defame them, stirring up the magistrates to suppress them; yet God was pleased to fill them with his living power, and give them such an open door of utterance in his service, that there was a mighty convincement over those parts.

He [George Fox] was a man that God endowed with a clear and wonderful depth, a discerner of others' spirits, and very much a master of his own.

In his testimony or ministry, he much laboured to open the truth to the people's understanding, and to bottom them upon the principle and principal, Christ Jesus, the Light of the World, that by bringing them to something that was of God in themselves, they might the better know and judge of him and themselves.

He had an extraordinary gift in opening the Scriptures. He would go to the marrow of things, and show the mind, harmony, and fulfilling of them with much plainness, and to great comfort and edification.

But above all he excelled in prayer. The inwardness and weight of his spirit, the reverence and solemnity of his address and behaviour, and the fewness and fullness of his words, have often struck, even strangers, with admiration, as they used to reach others with consolation.

He was of an innocent life, no busy-body, nor self-seeker, neither touchy nor critical. So meek, contented, modest, easy, steady, tender, it was a pleasure to be in his company. He exercised no authority but over evil, and that everywhere and in all; but with love, compassion and long-suffering. A most merciful man, as ready to forgive, as unapt to take or give an offence.

Thousands can truly say, he was of an excellent spirit and savour among them, and because thereof, the most excellent spirits loved him with an unfeigned and unfading love.

He was an incessant labourer; for in his younger time he laboured much in the word, and doctrine, and discipline in England, Scotland, and Ireland, turning many to God, and confirming those that were convinced of the truth. And between the years 1671 and 1677, he visited the churches of Christ in the plantations in America, and in the United Provinces and Germany, as his Journal relates, to the convincement and consolation of many.

I write my knowledge and my witness is true, having been with him for weeks and months together on divers occasions, and those of the nearest and most exercising nature, and that by night and by day, by sea and by land, in this and in foreign countries: and I can say I never saw him out of his place, or not a match for every service and occasion.

Thus he lived and sojourned among us: and as he lived, so he died; feeling the same eternal power, that had raised and preserved him, in his last moments. So full of assurance was he, that he triumphed over death; and so even in his spirit to the last, as if death were hardly worth notice or mention; recommending to some with him, the despatch and dispersion of an epistle, just before written to the churches of Christ throughout the world. But above all Friends, and of all Friends, those in Ireland and America, twice over saying, "Mine poor Friends in Ireland and America."

19

LIFE AT BATH

1700's

Oliver Goldsmith was the author of the novel the Vicar of Wakefield *as well as of the play* She Stoops to Conquer, *both of which are classics familiar to the English-speaking world today. He was, during his lifetime, a member of London's most exclusive literary circle. Known for his humanity and humor, he brought these qualities to bear in his description of "Life at Bath," one of the famous watering places of his day.*

LIFE AT BATH

by Oliver Goldsmith

Upon a stranger's arrival at Bath he is welcomed by a peal of the Abbey Bells, and in the next place, by the voice and music of the city waits [city musicians]. For these civilities, the ringers have generally a present made them of half-a-guinea, and the waits of half-a-crown, or more, in proportion to the person's fortune, generosity or ostentation. These customs, though disagreeable, are however, liked or they would not continue. The greatest incommodity attending them is the disturbance the bells must give the sick. But the pleasure of knowing the names of every family that comes to town recompenses the inconvenience. Invalids are fond of news, and upon the first sound of the bells everybody sends out to inquire for whom they ring.

After the family is thus welcomed to Bath, it is the custom for the master of it to go to the public places, and subscribe two guineas at the assembly-houses towards the balls and music in [the] pump-house, for which he is entitled to three tickets every ball night. His next subscription is a crown, half-a-guinea, or a guinea, according to his rank and quality, for the liberty of walking in the private walks belonging to Simpson's assembly-house; a crown or half-a-guinea is also given to the booksellers, for which the gentleman is to have what books he pleases to read at his lodgings, and at the coffee-house another subscription is taken for pen, ink, and paper, for such letters as the subscriber shall write at it during his stay. The ladies, too, may subscribe to the booksellers, and to a house by the pump-room, for the advantage of reading the news, and for enjoying . . . conversation.

Things being thus adjusted, the amusements of the day are generally begun by bathing, which is no unpleasing method of passing away an hour or so.

The baths are five in number. On the south-west side of the Abbey Church is the King's Bath, which is an oblong square; the walls are full of niches, and at every corner are steps to descend into it: this bath is said to contain 427 tons and 50 gallons of water; and on its rising out of the ground over the springs, it is sometimes too hot to be endured by those who bathe therein. Adjoining to the King's Bath, there is another, called the Queen's Bath; this is of a more temperate warmth, as borrowing its water from the other.

In the south-west part of the city are three other baths, viz: the Hot Baths, which is not much inferior in heat to the King's Bath, and contains 53 tons, 2 hogsheads, and 11 gallons of water; the Cross Bath, which contains 52 tons, 3 hogsheads, and 11 gallons; and the Leper's Bath, which is not so much frequented as the rest.

The hours for bathing are commonly between six and nine in the morning, and the baths are every morning supplied with fresh water; for when the people have done bathing, the sluices in each bath are pulled up, and the water is carried off by drains into the River Avon.

In the morning the lady is brought in a close chair, dressed in her bathing clothes, to the bath; and, being in the water, the woman who attends presents her with a little floating dish like a basin; into which the lady puts a handkerchief, a snuff-box, and a nosegay. She then traverses the bath; if a novice, with a guide; if otherwise, by herself; and having amused herself thus while she thinks proper, calls for her chair, and returns to her lodgings.

The amusement of bathing is immediately succeeded by a general assembly of people at the pump-room; some for pleasure, and some to drink the hot waters. Three glasses at three different times is the usual portion for every drinker; and the intervals between every glass are enlivened by the harmony of a small band of music, as well as by the conversation of the gay, the witty, or the forward.

From the pump-room the ladies, from time to time, withdraw to a female coffee-house, and from there return to their lodgings to breakfast. The gentlemen withdraw to their coffee-houses, to read the papers, or converse on the news of the day, with a freedom and ease not to be found in the metropolis.

People of fashion make public breakfasts at the assembly-houses, to which they invite their acquaintances, and they sometimes order private concerts; or, when so disposed, attend lectures on the arts and sciences, which are frequently taught there in a pretty superficial manner, so as not to tease the understanding, while they afford the imagination some amusement. The private concerts are performed in the ball-rooms; the tickets a crown each.

Concert breakfasts at the assembly-houses sometimes make also a part of the morning's amusement here, the expenses of which are defrayed by a subscription among the men. Persons of rank and fortune who can perform are admitted into the orchestra, and find a pleasure in joining with the performers.

Thus we have the tedious morning fairly over. When noon approaches, and church (if any please to go there) is done, some of the company appear upon the parade, and other public walks, where they continue to amuse each other, till they have formed parties for the play, cards, or dancing for the evening. Another part of the company divert themselves with reading in the booksellers' shops, or are generally seen taking the air and exercise, some on horseback, some in coaches. Some walk in the meadows round the town, winding along the side of the River Avon and the neighbouring canal; while others are seen scaling some of those romantic precipices that overhang the city.

When the hour of dinner draws nigh, and the company are returned from their different recreations, the provisions are generally served with the utmost elegance and plenty. Their mutton, butter, fish, and fowl, are all allowed to be excellent, and their cookery still exceeds their meat.

After dinner is over, and evening prayers ended, the company meet a second time at the pump-house. From this they retire to the walks, and from thence go to drink tea at the assembly-houses, and the rest of the evenings are concluded either with balls, plays, or visits. A theatre was erected in the year 1705, by subscription, by people of the highest rank, who permitted their arms to be engraven on the inside of the house, as a public testimony of their liberality towards it. Every Tuesday and Friday evening is concluded with a public ball, the contributions to which are so numerous, that the price of each ticket is trifling. Thus Bath yields a continual rotation of diversions, and people of all ways of thinking, even from the libertine to the methodist, have it in their power to complete the day with employments suited to their inclinations.

William Hogarth, one of England's famous artists, engraved this cartoon of the Theatre Royal Company performing at Covent Garden.

20

WHAT THE WELL-DRESSED WOMAN WEARS

1719

As early as 1719 the matter of competition for foreign trade, with which we are so familiar today, had become a problem in England.

In a paper written "In defense of the woolen manufacturers," an anonymous spinster lists the articles of clothing worn by a gentlewoman of the period, with a view to showing that most of them were of foreign origin.

Although this paper was written to protest the neglect of English goods, we enjoy today the picture it gives us of what the well-dressed Englishwoman wore in 1719.

WHAT A SPINSTER WEARS

I write myself SPINSTER, because the laws of my country call me so; and I think that name, used in all writings as the addition and distinction of a maiden or single woman on this island, denotes to us, that the general expectation of our lawgivers was, that the industry of female manufacturers would be most laudably employed this way, and therefore they gave the office of the Spinner as a title to the Gentlewoman.

In order to come at the true state of trade, and the interest of this island, with relation to the habits now worn, I shall take the modern English lady at eleven o'clock in the forenoon, which is her break of day: and allowing her until twelve for private devotion, suppose she has called to be dressed, and from the parcels of her dress, observing what she wears of English, and what of foreign product, with the prices of each part of her habit, make my references accordingly.

None amongst those whom we call *people of condition* can be at home or abroad, visit or receive visits, without having several dresses, with several suitable undresses, according to the following list, of absolute necessaries for a fine lady. She has now nothing on but her slippers, and her maid in calico clothes with the productions of the whole earth as under-written.

This is the necessary demand upon every gentleman, who would live in fashion and in quiet, for one dress for his lady: and as it would be scandalous (as his wife, anxious for his reputation, according to her duty, admonishes him) for her to be known by her clothes, she cannot but have five suits at least, and even with that she must stay at home one day in the week; but she is willing to do anything for her children and family, and would not appear abroad every day, like that flaring busybody her neighbour Mrs. Blank.

According to this rule, foreigners sell this lady to the value of a thousand pounds, where the English sell her to the value of five; and I believe any company or person, trade or trader, on the British side of the channel, will find it hard to balance this loss to our country by what they sell of English clothing to foreigners. I shall not therefore press the advantage further in the argument, so as to mention that her garters are French, and cost one pound five; that she has a pair of pockets of Marseilles quilting, which is another one pound five; nor need I observe that her stay-buckles, and buckles for her shoes, cannot be any other than brilliant, the price of which alters according to the price which others of our acquaintance, whom we love or envy, have purchased theirs. But I forgot that whatever part of the town the lady lives in, she must have a muff of five pounds five shillings; and if she lives in the city, she will catch cold if she has not a sable tippet worth fifteen pounds.

I had like to have concluded without taking notice, that the lining of her gown and petticoat was Italian lute-string, cheap

	£	s.	d.
A smock of cambrick holland, about three ells and a half, at 12 s. per ell	2	2	0
Marseilles quilted petticoat, three yards wide and a yard long.	3	6	0
An hoop petticoat covered with tabby	2	15	0
A French or Italian silk quilted petticoat, one yard and a quarter deep, and six yards wide.	10	0	0
A mantua and petticoat of French brocade, 26 yards, at three pounds per yard	78	0	0
A French point or Flanders laced head, ruffles and tucker	80	0	0
Stays covered with tabby, English	3	0	0
A French necklace	1	5	0
A Flanders laced handkerchief	10	0	0
French or Italian flowers for the hair	2	0	0
An Italian fan	5	0	0
Silk stockings, English	1	0	0
Shoes, English	2	10	0
A girdle, French	0	15	0
A cambrick pocket handkerchief	0	10	0
French kid gloves	0	2	6
A black silk alamode hood	0	15	0
A black French laced hood	5	5	0
Embroidered knot and bosom knot, French	2	2	0
Total	210	7	6

at eight pounds; but on the English side of the account, which I forgot when about her legs, it must be added that she had thread stockings worth ten shillings.

In an affair of this nature, wherein a great demand of things of small price rises to great profit, it must not be forgotten that the cap on which her head is dressed is of foreign silk, and so is the lace that ties it, as well as the lace for the stays. But for our encouragement at home, we supply her with pins, patches, powder, and wire. Patches may perhaps make a fraction in the account, therefore it must be considered that it is English labour upon Italian silk. I am dressing her for a visit; and as she is going out, she calls for her Turkey hankerchief, for which she gave five pounds five shillings; but she is now ready to move, and has called for either her coach or her chair; but as the maid is going, she bids her call both, lest she should alter her mind before she comes to the door, and then it is time enough to choose which of the vehicles she pleases.

21

A FOREIGNER'S VIEW OF ENGLAND

1725

The Quakers, or The Society of Friends, as they like to call themselves, are a sect that separated from the Church of England during the seventeenth century. Under the leadership of their founder, George Fox, they practiced a simple Christianity, even going out onto the street in their efforts to reach new converts—a method almost unheard of in those days.

In 1725, at the time of the young Swiss César de Saussure's visit to England, the influence of the Friends was spreading rapidly. And just as the tourist now delights in exploring strange cults in the countries on his itinerary, so at that time it was fashionable for the traveler from abroad to attend a Quaker meeting. Having watched the Quakers, as they were called because of their tremors during religious ecstasy, the visitor could return to his own country and regale his friends with his impressions.

But César de Saussure was also impressed by the unjust treatment to which English debtors were exposed. Eighty to one hundred thousand debtors thronged the English jails at this time with little or no hope of release. General Oglethorpe, founder of Georgia, had headed a committee to inspect English prisons. Like the young De Saussure, he too was shocked by the plight of these unfortunate men who owed debts they could never pay. He decided that a place of refuge must be found for them. In 1717

Parliament had created the new legal punishment of transporting to the New World certain types of prisoners, and from then on regular shipments of felons were dispatched to America.

Oglethorpe's Georgia, newest of the colonies, received the greatest number of these debtors, and gave them a chance to start a new life in a new world.

THE QUAKERS

by César de Saussure

The curious sect of Quakers, or Shakers, arose in the troubled times when England was torn by revolutions, anarchy and fanaticism, that is to say in the time of Cromwell. A rather crazy shoemaker's apprentice, George Fox, was the founder of this sect. It can almost be said that the Quakers form a particular nation of people, quite different from ordinary English citizens, by their language, manner of dressing, and religion.

Amongst their customs, one of which is thc use of the pronoun "thou," is that of never giving any man his titles, whatever his position or worth may be, for everyone to them is but a vile earthworm inhabiting this planet for a few years. Quakers make use of a sort of Bible talk, which strikes you more particularly, as it appears to date two hundred years back, no Bible having been printed in England in the fine modern language, the earliest edition of the Holy Book being still in use.

The Quakers' mode of dressing is as curious as their language; the men wear large, unlooped, flopping hats, without buttons or loops; their coats are as plain as possible, with no pleatings or trimmings, and no buttons or button-holes on the sleeves, pockets, or waists. If any brother were to wear ruffles to his shirts or powder on his hair, he would be considered impious. The most austere and zealous do not even wear shoe-buckles, but tie their shoes with cords. The women wear no ribbons, no lace, their gowns being of one modest color, without hoops, and their caps have no frills or pleatings, and are of a peculiar shape, made of silk and worn pleated on the forehead in a certain fashion particular to them. It must be owned, in truth, that this simple and modest attire suits many of these women admirably. Quakers' clothes, though of the simplest and plainest cut, are of excellent quality; their hats, clothes, and linen are of the finest, and so are the silken tissues the women wear. These people call each other "brother" and "sister," and to persons who are not of their sect they give the name of "friend"; they never make any compliments, and do not salute by taking off their hats or by making a curtsey.

All Quakers are merchants, and they never charge more for their goods than their worth. One day a young dandy, desirous of purchasing cloth for a coat, went into a Quaker's shop in London, and, seeing some cloth that suited his taste, he commenced haggling over the price of the merchandise. Finding that the Quaker would take nothing off the price of this article, the young man swore with an oath that he would not buy it at that price. At this the tradesman without a word folded up the cloth and put it away. The dandy proceeded to try various shops, but finding no cloth to suit him as well, either for price, color, or quality, as what he had first seen, he returned and asked for the cloth. The Quaker answered quietly, "Friend, thou didst swear thou wouldst not purchase my cloth at the price; as I can take nothing off, I cannot sell it thee, else I should be guilty of making thee swear a false oath; go and buy thy cloth elsewhere." Few merchants, I think, would have had the delicacy of feeling this Quaker merchant had.

Quakers claim to be Christians after the manner of the early members of the Church, but I do not know whether this appellation can really be given them, for they are never baptised. When a child is born the father or a near relative takes it up in his arms and says, "Welcome to this vale of misery." They declare they have communion with God, not with the lips but with the heart, and that communion was instituted to remind men of our Saviour's death, and that they, having His memory constantly before them, have no need of a reminder. Quakers have neither priests nor ministers, for they say it is not right that men should choose their own preacher. They are what we call inspired, and they consider themselves as machines made to move, act, and think by a Divine Providence.

I have attended some of their conventional assemblies. The meeting remains wrapped in profound silence, sometimes for as much as half an hour. The men's faces are hidden in the borders of their wide, flapping hats, which they never remove, and the women draw down their pretty silken caps or hide their faces with their fans. Everyone seems plunged in deep meditation, interrupted from time to time by a deep-drawn sigh, a groan, or a sob from some member of the assembly. Quakers also show their emotions by being taken with shaking fits, which make them appear to be suffering from fever, this latter characteristic being the origin of the name Quaker. Silence is at last suddenly interrupted by a brother jumping up, exclaiming, "The Spirit moves me," He repeats this phrase thrice, and then addresses his brethren in an incomprehensible jargon, repeating several times running those phrases he thinks most effective, and this is what this sect call preaching the gospel. When the first Quaker has finished his discourse another will rise in his stead, and sometimes several men and women will insist on being heard, declaring that they must speak, being inspired. These addresses are usually absurd; things worth listening to being intermingled with many that are not. This sect of Quakers tends to diminish every day, for amongst them are brethren anxious to taste of the honours of this life, and many youthful Quakers, whose fathers have died leaving them rich, have a longing to wear buttons on their sleeves and ruffles on their shirts, and to live after the fashion of other young men.

In Voltaire's time attention was focused on the strange dress and customs of the Quakers.

THE UNJUST LOT OF THE DEBTOR

by César de Saussure

In my humble opinion English laws are not sufficiently severe towards forgers and false witnesses, and too much so towards debtors, the latter being sent to prison; and as their maintenance is not paid for by the State, they must feed themselves. It is therefore easy to understand that many linger forever in prison suffering hunger and all manner of privations without hope of release, and unable to gain a livelihood which might free them. Magistrates are very hasty in issuing warrants and having debtors arrested. A creditor need only show a bill or present two witnesses who declare on oath that a person owes him a sum that he will not or cannot pay, the magistrate at once gives a warrant to a sort of sergeant called a bailiff, a person generally regarded by the people with great contempt. The bailiff is not permitted to arrest a debtor in his own house, or in any other. He therefore waylays him in the street, and producing his warrant and short staff of office, marches his prisoner off to the "Spunging House," where the latter is expected to regale the bailiff, his parasites, and friends with something to drink. The debtor remains a captive in his house for twenty-four hours; this in order to give him time to pay what he owes or to give bail. There are in London five or six prisons entirely for debtors. One of these is situated in the Fleet, and by a small payment prisoners obtain permission to make the whole quarter their prison, being however unable to leave it except under the penalty of being imprisoned anew. At this present time of writing from eighty to one hundred thousand debtors are imprisoned in London.

I must tell you of a singular adventure that befell a Flemish painter, a friend of mine, which will help to prove how easily the law allows the arrest of debtors. One day, in a coffee-house, the conversation turned on the imprisonment of debtors, and my friend the painter declared that he was fortunate enough to owe no man a penny, therefore no misfortune of the kind could ever befall him, and that this was lucky both for himself and his imaginary creditors, for were he once to be shut up in prison he could never hope to be released, as he would have lost his only means of livelihood. An Irishman who happened to be present, and had listened to the conversation, joined in, and declared that the painter, if imprisoned for debt, would have to bear it like everyone else, that he would quickly get over the shame, and no doubt would find means to pay the debt and to obtain his release. The painter and the Irishman left the coffee-house together. As soon as they were alone, the Irishman returned to the subject of debts, and the painter repeatedly declared that he was so afraid of imprisonment that he would take good care never to owe any man a single farthing. Some few weeks later the painter, who had in the meantime quite forgotten the conversation, was surprised and horrified at being one day stopped in the street by a bailiff, who produced a warrant, and ordered him to follow him to the Spunging House. Here he learnt that the scheming and rascally Irishman had brought two false witnesses to declare on oath that the painter owed him twenty guineas. My unfortunate friend, whose temper is very violent, swore and raged, and then sat down to think how best he could get out of this difficulty. He wrote to one of his friends, explaining his case, and begged him to help him by giving bail for him, thus enabling him to retain his freedom. This the friend consented to do, and the painter's next step was to endeavour to prove that the Irishman had lied. He went to law before the tribunal of the Marshalsea. The Irishman appeared with two false witnesses who swore that on such and such a day, at the Stock Exchange, the painter had borrowed twenty guineas from him, promising that he would return him the money in a fortnight. At the end of that time he was much troubled at not having been able to collect the necessary sum, for he had little credit, being a poor man. Suddenly he took a decision I should certainly never have taken. He resolved to pay out the Irishman in the same sort of coin as the supposed twenty guineas that had been lent him. He hired two other false witnesses who swore on oath that the painter had already repaid the debt. This led to a second law-suit, the painter being this time the gainer.

22

THE CUSTOM OF MAKING LOVE BY ADVERTISING

1737

At the invitation of a British nobleman, the Abbé Le Blanc came to England in 1737 and remained there seven years. A highly educated Frenchman of culture and sophisticated refinement, he perused the public advertisements tongue in cheek. The specimen of his journalistic research that follows throws an amusing light on the husband-hunting females of his day.

THE CUSTOM OF MAKING LOVE BY PUBLIC ADVERTISEMENTS

by Abbé Le Blanc

An English-woman takes a liking to some person in a place where she cannot reveal her mind to him. If he is a stranger and she knows not where to find him, she makes him a declaration of her passion in the public papers, describes him from head to foot that he may not mistake himself; puts him in mind of the time and place where she saw him; and appoints a meeting, if he chooses it. These news-papers are the greatest conveniences in the world. If a man wants to borrow money, or sell a horse, he advertises the public by this canal. For two shillings you may put in what advertisement you will: and they are of no less service for carrying on a love intrigue, than for recovering a lost snuff box. Here is an advertisement, which I read in yesterday's papers:

"If the young gentleman, who picked up a lady's handkerchief at St. Paul's last Tuesday, and advertised it in Wednesday's paper, is not married; and that he has the same sentiments in his heart, which she thought she read in his eyes; let him give an account of his substance, and a description of his person and qualifications, with a direction of the place of his usual residence: and the lady who [dropped] the handkerchief, will give him an opportunity to bring it back, and to aspire to greater favours."

You think perhaps that I joke, and exercise my imagination on a subject that may admit of it: but if you will not take my word, I have the very news-paper before me. I have likewise kept another published three months ago, which contains a much more singular advertisement. I give it word for word:

"This is to give notice to all persons whom it may concern, that a widow of between thirty and forty years of age, of a good family and considerable fortune, of a strong constitution, tho' fair; and as to figure passable at least; intends in the course of this month to deliver up her person and fortune to a man, in quality of her true and lawful husband, who has the following qualifications.

"First, it is required, that he be come to the age of maturity, that is, from twenty to five and twenty.

"Secondly, that he be of good constitution, which has not been hurt by debauchery, nor subject to the spleen, vapours, or any other melancholic disposition.

"Thirdly, he must be brown-haired and of a middle stature: she has reasons for not liking a man of too large a size, and thinks that the little is not always to be depended on. As to his face, it will be sufficient if he is not quite ugly: but she will absolutely reject an *Adonis,* because she would have a husband to herself alone.

"Fourthly, for worldly substance she desires none of him, provided he has all the other qualifications required. She does not so much as insist on his having been in France; if he is otherwise well-bred, good-natured, complaisant, and knows how to behave towards women. However upon an equality of all other circumstances, a person who has spent two years at Paris, shall have the preference.

"Fifthly, he must make outward profession at least of the established religion; for fear that a non-conformist, under pretence of tying his wife down to the severity of the gospel, should take it into his head to enslave her to his caprices, fix the hour and time to be spent on her toilet, retrench ornaments of dress, regulate her occupations, forbid her public diversions, and deprive her of lawful and fashionable amusements.

"Those who have any pretensions, are desired to send their names, and where they may be enquired after, in a letter sealed and put under cover to Mr. Tompson banker in Fleet-Street.

"N. B. Notice is given to all clergymen, tho' ever so young and conceited of their persons, not to give themselves any pains. The gentlemen of the black gown are excluded the lists, on account of the gloominess they generally spread in families.

"Smokers are likewise excepted against; because those who have contracted this nasty habit, either love not their own home, or bring bad company to it."

Let us not condemn the manners of our neighbours. If our *Police* tolerated such public advertisements, how many women would gladly take advantage of this method? and how many Paris writers would be found mean enough to become messengers and secretaries of such negotiations?

23

HOW THE WESLEY CHILDREN WERE BROUGHT UP

1732

John Wesley (1703–1791) was one of the greatest missionaries and religious organizers who ever lived. An ordained clergyman of the Church of England, he devoted his life to the poor and underprivileged, that underworld so graphically portrayed in the works of the great English artist William Hogarth. Wesley's revivalist doctrine, which preached that conversion comes as a sudden personal assurance of salvation, appealed to the multitudes. More than one hundred thousand adults, a proportion of the population of that time equal to half a million of the present number, became active members of his sect. John Wesley's religious movement was derisively called "methodism" because its adherents, its detractors said, laid so much stress on their revivalist methods. Wesley and his followers were untiring in preaching their gospel, even carrying their message as far as the American colonies, where Methodism became a powerful force.

Susanna Wesley, John's mother, was a woman of force and character. As her letter to her son shows very clearly, she had very definite and strict ideas on the rearing of children, which undoubtedly laid a firm foundation for his future career.

HOW THE WESLEYS WERE BROUGHT UP

by Susanna Wesley

July 24, 1732

Dear Son,

According to your desire, I have collected the principal rules I observed in educating my family; which I now send you as they occurred to my mind.

The children were always put into a regular method of living, in such things as they were capable of, from their birth; as in dressing, undressing, changing their linen, etc. The first quarter commonly passes in sleep. After that, they were, if possible, laid into their cradles awake, and rocked to sleep; and so they were kept rocking, till it was time for them to awake. This was done to bring them to a regular course of sleeping;

When turned a year old (and some before), they were taught to fear the rod, and to cry softly; by which means they escaped abundance of correction they might otherwise have had; and that most odious noise of the crying of children was rarely heard in the house; but the family usually lived in as much quietness as if there had not been a child among them.

As soon as they were grown pretty strong, they were confined to three meals a day. At dinner their little table and chairs were set by ours, where they could be overlooked; and they were suffered to eat and drink (small beer) as much as they would; but not to call for anything. If they wanted aught, they used to whisper to the maid which attended them, who came and spake to me; and as soon as they could handle a knife and fork, they were set to our table. They were never suffered to choose their meat, but always made to eat such things as were provided for the family.

At six, as soon as the family prayers were over, they had their supper; at seven, the maid washed them; and, beginning at the youngest, she undressed and got them all to bed by eight; at which time she left them in their several rooms awake; for there was no such thing allowed of in our house, as sitting by a child till it fell asleep.

They were so constantly used to eat and drink what was given them, that when any of them was ill, there was no difficulty in making them take the most unpleasant medecine; for they durst not refuse it, though some of them would presently throw it up. This I mention to show that a person may be taught to take anything, though it be never so much against his stomach.

In order to form the minds of children, the first thing to be done is to conquer their will, and bring them to an obedient temper. To inform the understanding is a work of time, and must with children proceed by slow degrees as they are able to bear it: but the subjecting the will is a thing which must be done at once; and the sooner the better. For by neglecting timely correction, they will contract a stubbornness and obstinacy which is hardly ever after conquered; and never without using such severity as would be as painful to me as to the child. In the esteem of the world they pass for kind and indulgent, whom I call cruel, parents, who permit their children to get habits which they know must be afterwards broken.

I insist upon conquering the will of children betimes, because this is the only strong and rational foundation of a religious education; without which both precept and example will be ineffectual. But when this is thoroughly done, then a child is capable of being governed by the reason and piety of its parents, till its own understanding comes to maturity, and the principles of religion have taken root in the mind.

The children of this family were taught as soon as they could speak the Lord's prayer, which they were made to say at rising and bed-time constantly; to which, as they grew bigger, were added a short prayer for their parents, and some collects; a short catechism, and some portion of Scripture, as their memories could bear.

They were very early made to distinguish the Sabbath from other days; before they could well speak or go. They were as soon taught to be still at family prayers, and to ask a blessing immediately after, which they used to do by signs, before they could kneel or speak.

They were quickly made to understand they might have nothing they cried for, and instructed to speak handsomely for what they wanted. They were not suffered to ask even the lowest servant for aught without saying, "Pray give me such a thing;" and the servant was chid, if she ever let them omit that word. Taking God's name in vain, cursing and swearing, profaneness, obscenity, rude, ill-bred names, were never heard among them. Nor were they ever permitted to call each other by their proper names without the addition of brother or sister.

For some years we went on very well. Never were children better disposed to piety, or in more subjection to their parents; till that fatal dispersion of them, after the fire, into several families. In those they were left at full liberty to converse with servants, which before they had always been restrained from; and to run abroad, and play with any children, good or bad. They soon learned to neglect a strict observance of the Sabbath, and got knowledge of several songs and bad things, which before they had no notion of. The civil behaviour which made them admired when at home, by all which saw them, was, in great measure, lost; and a clownish accent, and many rude ways, were learned, which were not reformed without some difficulty.

When the house was rebuilt, and the children all brought home, we entered upon a strict reform; and then was begun the custom of singing psalms at beginning and leaving school, morning and evening. Then also that of a general retirement at five o'clock was entered upon; when the oldest took the youngest that could speak, and the second the next to whom they read the Psalms for the day, and a chapter in the New Testament; as, in the morning, they were directed to read the Psalms and a chapter in the Old: after which they went to private prayers, before they got their breakfast, or came into the family. And I thank God, the custom is still preserved among us.

24

AN EVENING AT THE TAVERN

1755

Samuel Johnson, writer and critic, was one of the great figures of the age in which he lived (1709–1784). His famous dictionary, on which he worked for eight years, was published in 1755.

As large in intelligence as in stature, he loved good food, good liquor, and good conversation. In the excerpt that follows we see a candid portrait not only of Johnson himself but of the coffeehouse life so typical of the times.

AN EVENING AT THE DEVIL'S TAVERN WITH DR. JOHNSON

by A Young Surgeon

Late home last night from an evening with my three friends. At the Infirmary in the afternoon. . . . Then we four feeling in the mood for Levity did wander through the streets entering the City by the gates of Ludgate and so into that road called Fleet Street, a very famous road the haunts of both wits and roués.

We entered the Devil's Tavern which is the Second house, and a great resort of Physicians, many meeting here for a pleasant philosophical discourse, to find it very crowded many people coming and going. On enquiring the reason of the Host he did inform us that that night one famous Johnson, a famous novelist known to his friends as the "Doctor," was giving a dinner in honour of a Mrs. Lennox who had published her first novel, "The Life of Harriet Stuart," he and the members of his club coming there from their usual meeting place in Ivy Lane, Paternoster Row.

George Blumenfield did catch sight of one Doctor Bathurst then entering and he knowing him to introduce us; and as we talked a monstrous fat man afflicted with a dropsy and with a great broad face came in with a lady on his arm. He bids Doctor Bathurst good evening in a voice sonorous though pleasant and smiling round on us, did ask whether we were perhaps relations of the Doctor [Bathurst]; the which the Doctor did deny. "Then, sirs," said the fat man, "Ye are brothers with him in the search for knowledge?" to which George replies that we are Surgeons in Embryo formed but not delivered, at the which the fat man laughs and further enquiring our business does then bid us to join his gathering; the which I took kindly of him. He presents the Lady to us, she being we learn that Mrs. Lennox of whom the worthy landlord had spoken; and he, Dr. Bathurst, informs us in a whisper, the great Johnson himself. And so in agreeable converse we go upstairs into a large upper room very gay with many candles on a great table, and the Doctor received with shouts of acclamation from some gentlemen drinking wine before a great fire of logs. Doctor Bathurst introduces us to other physicians. He informs us that we are fortunate indeed to have been admitted into such a company, for Johnson's Club is the most famous in London town and likely long to be remembered, the Doctor now engaged upon a great Dictionary and already notable from having published a poem, "The Vanity of Human Wishes," of which even His Majesty has well-spoken, and a Magazine, "The Rambler," which is published twice weekly.

The Doctor was established in a great chair at the head of the table and the gentlemen all grouped themselves along it. Mrs. Lennox being seated at his right hand in a chair that with a pleasant conceit the Doctor had caused to be draped with Regal Purple, and we four found ourselves chairs at the end of the table. My seat being near the door, thereby intolerably draughty but of satisfaction since it afforded me a good view of the Doctor. The Doctor being seated did call for silence and then pouring a glass of wine, said that his Physician had forbidden him wine but that in honour of the occasion he would dare to take a preparatory glass both for the good of his Digestion and for the Honour of the Lady who sat by him; and then helped by Doctor M'Ghie and one Hawkins, an attorney, he did rise to his feet and tender to the Lady his very humble admiration, holding out the glass to her and bowing with his shoulders and head; at which all the gentlemen rose to their feet toasting the lady with many warm little speeches of respectful admiration, she blushing and laughing and crying all at once. Then they seated themselves again and the waiters did bring in their supper.

Amongst these dishes that I remember were:

- A dish of rabbits all smothered with onions.
- A leg of mutton boiled with capers and served with walnuts and melted butter.
- A side of beef with frizzled potatoes.
- A roasted goose with some chickens and other game.
- A roasted lobster, served with cunning with all his claws arranged as though alive.
- A dish of fish with their bellies stuffed with pudding.

And a currant pudding and a vast Apple Pie, this last especially ordered by the Doctor who growing merry did wish to adorn it with Bay Leaves as a compliment to Mrs. Lennox who is a Poetess. But she laughingly demurring that they wish to spoil the flavor of the Pie, he to produce a crown of Laurel Leaves that he had prepared and with this to crown her, the company all crying out and laughing at this pretty conceit.

We did drink wine and ale according to our taste with the Meat, but the Doctor kept to Lemonade which though a foully sharp beverage did not seem to sharpen his temper. About eleven of the clock the remnants of the food were cleared away and nuts and fruit set out and coffee served; some of the gentlemen left being overcome with the heat of the room and the potency of the wines. I did feel somewhat foxed myself and on looking around did see that Mr. St. Clair was leaving and that Mr. Pope had already left; but did later find him beneath the table. The Doctor, our host, had eaten I do believe more than anyone else in the room; I did marvel at the way he crammed all manner of meats into his mouth until his face became purple and the veins stood out on his temples, but he seemed to suffer no inconvenience from it, his face now shining with sweat and merriment until it resembled a Full Moon. Moreover he never ceased talking, and the flow of his discourse flowed on like a river, the sonorous timber of his voice drowning all who interrupted him. So to my feet and to take a cup of coffee which Arabian drink did clear my head. And so, feeling infernally sleepy and fuddled, did awake George B. who had gone to sleep with his feet on the table, and out with him into the Street. And so home to our beds with all speed, for fear of the Night Hawks that do infest the streets at these hours.

25

BLACKSTONE'S COMMENTARIES

1760's

In 1922 the American Bar Association presented to the people of Great Britain a statue of a famous British jurist, the author of the renowned Commentaries on the Laws of England. *The object of this gift was to acknowledge publicly the debt that the United States' legal system owes to William Blackstone.*

Following the American Declaration of Independence, Blackstone's Commentaries *became the bible on which American jurisprudence was founded. Even today no law library is complete without the volumes of Blackstone.*

William Howard Taft, former Chief Justice and President of the United States, voiced the common reverence felt by all American lawyers for the remarkable English giant of jurisprudence when he said:

"I feel strangely moved finding myself sitting here [in the Middle Temple] in the home of Blackstone, in the very cradle of the Common Law of England and America."

William Blackstone was born in London in 1723, the son of a prosperous London merchant. At the age of fifteen he entered Pembroke College, Oxford. After studying law in the Middle Temple, he was called to the bar in 1746. Unsuccessful as a practicing trial attorney, he found his place in the legal world as a lecturer in law at Oxford. His talent for lucid statement and intel-

lectual analysis was matched by his understanding of the human meaning of the law.

Perhaps America's debt to England has never been more clearly demonstrated than in the adoption of the fundamental principles of English common law which, as laid down in the pages of Blackstone's Commentaries, *give to every individual impartial justice and equal protection.*

FROM AN ABRIDGEMENT OF BLACKSTONE'S COMMENTARIES IN A SERIES OF LETTERS TO HIS DAUGHTER.

(printed 1822 by John Hatchard & Sons, London)

My dear E:

It is not unlikely that many persons who have never opened Blackstone's Commentaries on the Laws of England will think that I am unreasonable in requiring a young lady to read a book which treats of a subject plainly uninteresting and probably unintelligible. Believe me, those who have formed this opinion have adopted it without sufficient consideration. While I would avoid, in formal education, the two extremes of pedantic learning and of mere superficial accomplishments, I would wish to adorn your mind with useful knowledge and with such literary acquirements as will render you a cheerful companion and an accomplished woman.

It is for a similar purpose that I now send you, in a series of letters, so much of the Commentaries on the Laws of England as I think are adapted to your understanding, as well as necessary to be known by every gentlewoman.

I can safely pronounce that, with some exceptions, all the historical parts of the laws of England are within reach of any capacity and you will find, in the course of this correspondence that most of those subjects which I shall explain to you in detail, will be recognised by you as interwoven in the history of your country and of which you have had already general ideas.

There is no person, let his rank, fortune or profession be what it may, but will derive at once amusement, instruction and advantage from the knowledge of those laws, under which he enjoys the blessings of protection and of impartial justice.

But I need not impress upon you that all knowledge must be advantageous which renders you better informed, which affords material for reflection and opens an additional source of mental occupation and improvement. If that knowledge is on a subject of every-day occurrence; if it gives you an insight into those institutions, customs and regulations which are constantly presenting themselves to your notice; if it explains satisfactorily what otherwise would be confused, and exposes in genuine simplicity what otherwise would be clothed in darkness and mystery; then indeed you will have obtained an acquisition which will be an inexhaustible source of pleasure and profit; and the benefit of which will be felt in all the concerns of life; it will teach you to be just to others, as you require justice yourself; to pity and assist your fellow creatures; to make allowance for their feelings; and to thank God that you are removed from those temptations and trials to which others less fortunate, are so often exposed and so often fall miserable victim.

These are some of the grounds on which I wish you to become acquainted with the laws of your country; and I will, as leisure permits from time to time send you a chapter of Blackstone's Commentaries abridged in the best manner I can.

I remain,

Your loving father.

(undated)

26

THE GREATEST FAIR IN EUROPE

1750's

The county fair has always been a popular event for the exchange of gossip and the selling and buying of all sorts of wares from books to livestock.

As late as the eighteenth century, Stourbridge Fair was the most important in Europe, comparable to the great fairs of the present time.

In addition to the actual business accomplished, there was, as is the custom today, a great deal of eating and drinking; and the roast goose and boiled pork of that era were possibly better tasting than today's hot dogs and hamburgers.

THE GREATEST FAIR IN EUROPE

by Edmund Carter

The Fair which was thought some years ago to be the greatest in Europe, is kept in a cornfield about half a mile square, having the River Cam running in the north side thereof, and the rivulet called the Stour on the east side: and it is about two miles east of Cambridge market-place, where, during the Fair, coaches, chaises, and chariots attend to carry persons to the Fair.

The shops, or booths, are built in rows like streets, having each their name—as Garlic Row, Bookseller's Row, Cook Row, etc.

And every commodity has its proper place—as the Cheese Fair, Hop Fair, Wool Fair, etc. And here, as in several other streets or rows, are all sorts of traders, who sell by wholesale or retail—as goldsmiths, toy-men, brasiers, turners, milliners, haberdashers, hatters, mercers, drapers, pewterers, China warehouses; and, in a word, most trades that can be found in London, from whence many of them come.

Here are also taverns, coffee-houses, and eating-houses in great plenty; and all kept in booths, in any of which (except the coffee booth) you may at any time be accommodated with hot or cold roast goose, roast or boiled pork, etc.

Crossing the main road at the south end of Garlic Row, and a little to the left hand, is a great square, formed by the largest booths, called the Duddery, the area of which Square is from 240 to 300 feet, chiefly taken up with woolen drapers, wholesale tailors, and sellers of second-hand clothes: where the dealers have room before their booths to take down and open their packs, and bring in wagons to load and unload the same.

In the Centre of this Square was (till within these three years) erected a tall Maypole, with a vane on top; and in this square, on the two chief Sundays during the Fair, both forenoon and afternoon, Divine Service is read, and a sermon preached from a pulpit placed in the open air, by the Minister of Barnwell; who is very well-paid for the same by the contributions of the Fair-keepers.

In this Duddery only, it is said, there have been sold £100,000 worth of woolen manufactures in less than a week's time; beside the prodigious trade carried on here by the wholesale tailors from London, and most other parts of England, who transact their business wholly in their pocket-books, and meeting here their chap-men from all parts, make up their accounts, receive money chiefly in bills, and take further orders.

These, they say, exceed by far the sale of goods actually brought to the Fair, and delivered in kind; it being frequent for the London wholesale men to carry back orders from their dealers for £10,000 worth of goods a man, and some much more.

And once in this Duddery, it is said, there was a booth consisting of six apartments all belonging to a dealer in Norwich stuffs only, who had there above £20,000 worth of these goods.

The trade for wool, hops, and leather here is prodigious: the quantity of wool only sold at one fair is said to have amounted to £50,000 or £60,000; and of hops very little less.

The Fair is like a well-governed city; and less disorder and confusion to be seen there than in any other place where there is so great a concourse of people.

Here is a Court of Justice always open from morning till night where the Mayor of Cambridge or his deputy sits as judge, determining all controversies in matters arising from the business of the Fair, and seeing the Peace thereof kept; for which purpose he hath eight servants, called Red-coats, one or other of which are constantly at hand in most parts of the Fair.

If any dispute arise between buyer and seller, on calling out "Red-coat," you have instantly one or more come running to you; and if the dispute is not quickly decided, the offender is carried to the said Court, where the case is decided in a summary way, from which Sentence there lies no appeal.

27

THE DIARY OF THOMAS TURNER

1750's

Thomas Turner was born on June 9, 1729. His diary, which covers most of his life, gives a simple but graphic account of village life during the reign of George II. Thomas Turner, a shopkeeper at East Hoathly in the county of Sussex, is not a figure of any historical importance. He lives quietly, marries, drinks too much and too often. His wife dies and he marries again. A sensible, human person, he takes little interest in the sociological events of his time. But today his diary is interesting for its contemporary report of what people in a small Sussex village during the eighteenth century were thinking about—what they were reading, what they ate, what they hoped for, and what they feared. This is history as seen by the little man.

THE DIARY OF THOMAS TURNER

Sunday, Feb. 8, 1754.—As I by experience find how much more conducive to my health, as well as pleasantness and serenity of my mind, to live in a low, moderate rate of diet, and as I know I shall never be able to comply ther[e]with in so strict a manner as I should chuse, by the unstable and over-easyness of my temper, I think it therefore fit to draw up Rules of proper Regimen, which I do in the manner and form following, which I hope I shall always have the strictest regard to follow, as I think they are not inconsistent with either religion or morality.

If I am at home, or in company abroad, I will never drink more than four glasses of strong beer: one to toast the King's health, the second to the Royal Family, the third to all friends, and the fourth to the pleasure of the company. If there is either wine or punch, never upon any terms or persuasion to drink more than eight glasses, each glass to hold no more than half a quarter of a pint.

October 15.—My wife and I having fixed to go to Hartfield, my wife endeavoured to borrow a horse of Jos. Fuller, Tho. Fuller, Will Piper, and Jos. Burgess, to no purpose, they having no reason for not doing it, but want of good nature and a little gratitude; tho' I make no doubt but they will, some or other of them, be so good-natured as soon to come and say, 'Come, do write this land-tax or window-tax book for us'; then I will always find good nature enough to do it, and at the same time to find them in beer, gin, pipes, and tobacco; and then poor ignorant wretches, they sneak away and omit to pay for their paper; but, God bless them, I'll think it proceeds more from ignorance than ill nature.

My wife having hired a horse of John Watford, [Almost the only mode of getting about in Sussex in those days was on horseback, the husband riding with his wife on a pillion behind him.] about four o'clock we set out on our journey for Hartfield, and as we were riding along near to Hastingford, no more than a foot's pace, the horse stood still, and continued kicking-up until we was both off, in a very dirty hole (but, thanks be to God, we received no hurt). My wife was obliged to go to Hastingford House, to clean herself. My wife and I spent the even at my father Slater's. We dined off some ratios of pork and green salad.

Friday, Aug. 12.—This day being the first race-day at Lewes, my sister Ann Slater and I upon a horse borrowed of Mr. French, rode to Lewes, where we arrived just as the people came from the hill. We went to see the ball, which, in my opinion, was an extreme pretty sight. The King's plate of 100 sovereigns was run for by Mr. Warren's horse Careless, and Mr. Roger's horse Newcastle Jack, which was won by Careless, the other being drawn after the first heat. 'Tis said there were £100 laid by the grooms that Careless beat the other six score yards, which he did.

Sept. 18.—My whole family at church—myself, wife, maid, and the two boys. We dined off a piece of boiled beef and carrots, and currant suet pudding; and we had, I think, too extreme good sermons this day preached unto us.

Tuesday, Oct. 11.—My brother and I set out for Battle market. I think Battle to be a pleasant situated town, and there seems to be a considerable market for stock; and the Abbey—which belongs to the family of the Websters and which was built just after the Conquest, in memory of the battle fought near that place between the Conqueror and Harold, in which the latter, his two brothers, most of the English nobility, and 97,974 common men (!) were killed—is the remains of a fine Gothic structure.

Sunday, Dec. 25th.—Myself, the two boys, and servant at church; I and the maid staid the Communion. This being Christmas-day, the widow Marchant, Hannah, and James Marchant, dined with us on a buttock of beef and a plumb suet pudding. Tho. Davy at our house in the even, to whom I read two nights of the 'Complaint,' one of which was 'Christian's Triumph against the Fear of Death': a noble subject, it being the redemption of mankind by Jesus Christ. I think the author has treated it in a very moving and pathetic manner.

1757, Jan. 9.—Mr. Eless, Marchant, myself and wife, sat down to whist about seven o'clock, and played all night: very pleasant, and, I think I may say, innocent mirth, there being no oaths nor imprecations sounding from side to side, as is too often the case at cards.

Aug. 19.—I entertained my sister Sally, and my brother's wife, with the sight of the modern microcosm, which I think is a very pretty curious sight, for we see the whole solar system move by clockwork, in the same manner they do in the heavens.

Aug. 23.—About four P.M., I walked down to Halland with several more of my neighbours, in order for a rejoicing for the taking of Cape Breton, etc., where there was a bonfire of six hundred faggots, the cannon fired, and two barrels of beer given to the populace, and a very good supper provided for the principle tradesmen of this and neighbouring parishes, as there had been a dinner for the gentlemen of Lewes and the neighbouring parishes. After supper we drank a great many loyall healths, and I came home in a manner quite sober. There was I believe, near one hundred people entertained at Halland this day, besides the populace, and, so far as I see, everything was carried on with decency and regularity; tho' I must think the most proper way of rejoicing is by having a general thanksgiving, that the whole nation may give thanks to Him that gives success to our armies, both by sea and land; and I think to show our outward joy, it might be more properly done by distributing something to the poor.

Oct. 20 [1759].—In the even, read the 'Extraordinary Gazette' for Wednesday, which gives an account of our Army in America, under the command of General Woolf, beating the French army under General Montcalm, near the city of Quebec, wherein both the generals were killed, as also two more French generals; as also the surrender of the city of Quebec. Oh, what a pleasure it is to every true Briton, to see with what success it pleases Almighty God to bless his Majesty's arms, they having success at this time in Europe, Asia, Africa, and America!

July 9 [1760].—In the afternoon my wife walked to Whitesmith, to see a mountebank perform wonders, who has a stage built there, and comes once a week to cuzen a parcel of poor deluded creatures out of their money, by selling his packets, which are to cure people of more distempers than ever they had in their lives, for 1 s. each, by which means he takes sometimes £8 or £9 of a day.

Tuesday, Oct. 7.—In the even there was a rejoicing at Halland, and a bonfire, for our army under the command of General Amherst having taken Montreal and all Canada from the French. All the neighbo[u]rhood was regaled with a supper, wine, punch, and strong beer.

Sunday, Oct. 26.—To-day we had the melancholy news of the death, by a fit of the apoplexy of his most august Majesty George II., king and parent of this our most happy isle; had his Majesty lived to the 10th of November, he would have been seventy-seven years of age. He has sit upon the British throne thirty-three years the 22nd of last June.

28

SOME RULES

FOR A WELL-BRED GENTLEMAN

1762-1768

For over three hundred years Lord Chesterfield has been the recognized social mentor on both sides of the Atlantic, an authority on how "the well-bred gentleman" conducts himself in society. His letters to his adopted son and heir do not restrict themselves to the outer courtesies. Urbane and highly civilized, Lord Chesterfield was above all a wise and experienced man. He stressed the fundamental need of a human being to live at peace with himself. Having achieved this, he would almost naturally reflect his inner ease in a social posture that would make him both admired and loved.

In spite of the great differences in social customs brought about by the spread of democracy, Lord Chesterfield's view of life is still relevant to the more relaxed and informal social pattern of our time.

SOME RULES FOR THE BEHAVIOR OF A WELL-BRED GENTLEMEN

by Philip Dormer, Fourth Earl of Chesterfield

1762

Dear Phil,

As I know that you desire to be a well-bred Gentleman, and not a two-legged Bear, and to be beloved, instead of being hated or laughed at, I send you some general rules for your behaviour, which will make you not only be loved but admired. You must have great attention to everything that passes where you are, in order to do what will be most agreeable to the company.

Whoever you speak to, or whoever speaks to you, you must be sure to look them full in the face. For it is not only ill-bred, but brutal, either to look upon the ground, or to have your eyes wandering about the room, when people are speaking to you, or you are speaking to them. When people speak to you, though they do not directly ask you a question, you must give them an answer, and not let them think that you are deaf, or that you do not care what they say. For example if a person says to you *this is a very hot day,* you must say, yes or no Sir.

You must call every gentleman, Sir, or My Lord, and every Woman, Madam.

You must never on any account put your fingers in your nose, for that is excessively ill-bred, very nasty, and will make your nose bleed and be very sore. What is your handkerchief for?

When you are at dinner you must sit upright in your chair, and not loll. And when anybody offers to help you to anything if you will have it you must say, *yes if you will be so good,* or *I am ashamed to give you so much trouble.* If you will not have it, you must say, *no thank you,* or *I am very much obliged to you.* You must drink first to the Mistress of the House and next to the Master of it.

When you first come into a room you must not fail to make a bow to the company, and also when you go out of it.

You must never look sullen or pouting, but have a cheerful, easy countenance.

Remember that there is no one thing so necessary for a Gentleman as to be perfectly civil and well-bred; nobody was ever loved that was not well-bred; and to tell you the truth neither your Papa nor I shall love you, if you are not well-bred, and I am sure you desire that we should both love you, as we do now, because you are a very good boy. And so God bless you.

Black-Heath June 28th 1768

My Dear Boy,

Mr. Addison in the 243d 'Spectator' says very truly that the two great ornaments of Virtue are cheerfulness and goodnature, to which I will add that they are not only the ornaments but the effects of virtue. He adds that a man cannot be agreeable who is not easy within himself. This truth I am sure you have felt in your own little experience. Recollect those days when you have not done what you should do, and have been rebuked by Dr. Dodd, have you been easy or cheerful? Or rather have you not felt an uneasy consciousness and an awkward gloomyness? On the contrary when you have done your business well, and received the Doctor's applause, have you not found yourself remarkably cheerful and lightsome? These sentiments you will experience upon a much larger scale when you are grown to be a Man, and have a more extensive power of doing good; and I am so convinced of the goodness of your little heart, that I am sure as it grows bigger it will only be the fuller of benevolence. Nay, I will venture to prophesy that you will reckon those days the happiest of your life in which you have done the most good. Those feelings are exquisite, and a Man who would lead a life of pleasure, will despise all others. Titus, who is known by the name of the good Emperor, used to say that he had lost a day when he had done no good in it; for this he was justly styled, *Deliciae humani generis* [delights of mankind], and was the only ruler that ever I read of, who deserved that glorious title. You may if you please, and I verily believe you will, be called *Deliciae societatis humanae* [delights of human society]. When you see any person in company pensive, dark, gloomy, and taking no part, except sometimes a snarling one, take it for granted that all is not right within. Some mean passion, such as envy, avarice, or hatred, engrosses his breast, and leaves no room for the agreeable social feelings. *Nihil conscire sibi nulla; pallescere culpa* [Horace, Epistle I, 1. 61, to be conscious to himself of no ill: to turn pale with no fault], is a sure receipt for good humor, which in the common intercourse of life is not only useful but necessary, especially when you come to be in great business; it gives graces to favors and softens refusals; it prevents those disagreeable *Absences* or *Distractions*, which many people are apt to fall into, for it gives the heart and mind their full play. God bless thee.

To Mr. Stanhope
at Dr. Dodd's at Whitton, near Twickenham, in Middlesex.

29

DIARY OF A YOUNG LADY OF FASHION

1764-1765

The streets of London in 1764 were even more hazardous than are the streets of our large cities today. They were dark and infested with pickpockets, footpads, and mounted highwaymen. Horace Walpole, writing to a friend, remarked, "One is forced to travel even at noon as if one were going to battle."

In her diary a young lady of fashion describes both the London of her day and the holdup to which she was subjected. Two hundred years have passed since then, but unfortunately the twentieth-century crime wave does not differ markedly from that of the eighteenth century.

THE STREETS OF LONDON

May 22, 1764

"Carrots and Turnips Ho!" This cry, yelled in a hoarse voice wakes me every morning. My father complains of the noise of London, and, indeed, 'tis monstrous. The watchmen are calling out the time and weather all night long, and when they have stopped the vendors of oranges, brooms, matches, rat-traps, Lord

Many English streets, like this one, had not yet been paved with cobblestones by the mid-eighteenth century. They became seas of mud when it rained.

knows what else begin. For my part I find it very enlivening, but I am not surprised that the town ladies are as thin as Maypoles.

Am still much confused with this new house and the many new domestics, whom I have put in Mrs. S's charge. My father has bought me a very elegant sedan chair with four bearers. It is to be at my disposition whenever I wish to go out, and I intend to furnish it with rose satin cushions and curtains. Seated in it and wearing my rose brocade, I flatter myself I shall be an elegant sight.

I am amazed at the vastness of this town and the bustle of coaches and chairs in the street.

June 18, 1764

I spend half the day at the hairdresser's now. My head has not been opened for over a fortnight, and this is positively the longest time I will go in this hot weather, though some ladies keep their heads unopened till they are intolerable to themselves and everyone else. The dresser informed me that one lady, from motives of thrift, went so long a time that her head, when opened, was found to contain a nest of mice. Lord save me from that!

June 23rd.

An odious and utterly unexpected mishap occurred to me last night! Was returning with Lady D. from the play in her coach. 'T'was a dark, rainy night. As we passed through St. James Square our horses stopped suddenly, there was a noise of scuffling and shouts, the window was pulled open, and a masked ruffian thrust his head in and presented a pistol at our breasts with the words "Dames, stand and deliver—off with those jewels now." Words cannot depict our fright and consternation. Lady D. in her anger swore like a trooper, and I very rashly attempted to jump out of the coach and call for the watchman. A pistol held against my very bosom made me realise the hopeless position we were placed in. Weeping with rage and vexation, I removed my jewels while Lady D. did likewise. The villain then gallopped away. I lay the night at Lady D's house, being too agitated to return home, and we spent half the night in fruitless lamentations.

30

CHILDREN'S WORKHOUSES AND THE PRISONS

1770's

Most of the children who were sent to the London workhouse were vagrants, orphans, or destitute children dependent for their support on the local parish.

Although living conditions in the workhouse were Spartan to the point of hardship, the children did receive some instruction. They were taught spinning of wool and flax, sewing, knitting, and winding silk. They were also trained to make their own clothes and shoes. In addition, they received some elementary instruction in reading, writing, and arithmetic.

In 1770 the English prisons were indeed a disgrace to the nation. Not only did adult prisoners, many of whom were confined for relatively small debts, live under appalling sanitary conditions but, in their depleted state, they fell victim by the hundreds to a malignant illness known as jail fever.

John Howard, the first great prison reformer, was forty-seven years old when, on his appointment as Sheriff of Bedford, he saw, for the first time, the terrible conditions existing in the prisons. From then until the day of his death in 1790, his life was dedicated to the cause of prison reform.

After visiting some two hundred English prisons, he wrote a graphic and detailed report on the horrors he had seen. His book, The State of the Prisons, *was first published in 1777. It went into three editions, awakened the conscience of a nation to the claims of an inarticulate and forgotten minority, and brought about long-overdue reforms.*

DAILY LIFE IN THE CHILDREN'S WORKHOUSE

by Hatton

The Bell rings at 6 o'clock in the Morning to call up the Children, and half an Hour after, the Bell is rung for Prayers, and Breakfast; at 7 the Children are set to work; 20 under a Mistress to spin Wool and Flax, to Knit Stockings, to wind Silk, to make and Sew their Linen, Cloaths, Shoes, Mark, etc. All the Children are called down for an Hour every Day to Read, and an Hour every day to Write, 20 at a time.

At 12 o'clock they go to Dinner, and have a little time to play till One, then they are set to work again till 6 o'clock. They are rung to Prayers, to their Supper, and allowed to play till Bed time.

Every Nurse combs her Children with a small tooth comb 3 times a Week; mends the Children's Clothes; makes their beds, washes their Wards; and sees the Children go neat and clean, and that they wash and comb themselves every day.

Some Children earn ½d., some 1d. and some 4d. per day.

The Children are taught their *Catechism,* and often Catechised by the Minister, especially every Sunday.

When Children are grown up to 12, 13 or 14 years of Age they are put forth Apprentices to Masters of Ships, and other Sea faring Men, and to Handycraft Trades and others and the Governors give them a good ordinary Suit of Clothes or 20s. in Money at the Election of the Master or Mistress.

The Seal or Badge of this Corporation is an Orphan, his Left Hand resting on the Head of a Sheep, with this Motto, *God's Providence is our Inheritance.*

THE STATE OF THE PRISONS

by John Howard

There are prisons, into which whoever looks will, at first sight of the people confined, be convinced, that there is some great error in the management of them; their sallow meager countenances declare, without words, that they are very miserable. Many, who went in healthy, are in a few months changed to emaciated dejected objects. Some are seen pining under diseases "sick and in prison"; expiring on the floors, in loathsome cells, of pestilential fevers, and the confluent smallpox; victims, I must not say to the cruelty, but I will say to the inattention of sheriffs, and gentlemen in the commission of the peace.

Some keepers of these houses, who have represented to the magistrates the wants of their prisoners, and desired for them necessary food, have been silenced with these inconsiderate words, "Let them work or starve."

In consequence of this, at the quarter sessions you see prisoners covered (hardly covered) with rags; almost famished; and sick of diseases, which the discharged spread where they go; and with which those . . . sent to the county gaols infect these prisons.

Many prisons have no water. This defect is frequent in bridewells and county gaols. In some places where is water, prisoners are always locked up within doors, and have no more than the keeper or his servant think fit to bring them; in one place they were limited to three pints a day each.

And as to air, methods are contrived to rob prisoners of this genuine cordial of life by preventing that circulation and change of the salutiferous fluid, without which animals cannot . . . thrive.

My reader will judge of its malignity, when I assure him that my clothes in my first journeys became so offensive, that in a post-chaise I could not bear the window drawn up; and was therefore obliged to travel commonly on horseback. The leaves of my memorandum book were often so tainted, that I could not use it till after spreading it an hour or two before the fire; and even my antidote, a vial of vinegar, has, after using it in a few prisons, become intolerably disagreeable. One cause why the rooms in some prisons are so close, is the window-tax, which the gaolers have to pay; this tempts them to . . . stifle the prisoners.

I am ready to think that none who give credit to what is contained in the foregoing pages, will wonder at the havoc made by the gaol-fever. In 1773, 1774 and 1775 I was fully convinced that many more prisoners were destroyed by it, than were put to death by all the public executions in the kingdom.

But the mischief is not confined to prisons. Not to mention now the number of sailors, and of families in America, that have been infected by transports—multitudes caught the distemper by going to their relatives and acquaintance in the gaols; many others from prisoners discharged, and not a few in the courts. . . .

In Baker's Chronicle, that historian mentioning the assize held in Oxford Castle 1577 (called from its fatal consequence the black assize) informs us, that "all who were present died within forty hours; the lord chief baron, the sheriff and about three hundred more. Lord Chancellor Bacon ascribes this to a disease brought into court by the prisoners. . . .

At the Lent assize in Taunton 1730, some prisoners who were brought thither from Ivelchester gaol, infected the court; and Lord Chief Baron Pengelly; Sir James Sheppard, sergeant; John Pigot Esq., sheriff, and some hundreds besides, died of the gaol-distemper. The numbers that were carried off by the same malady in London in 1750, two judges, the lord mayor, one alderman, and many of inferior rank, are too well known to . . . mention.

In many gaols there is no allowance of bedding or straw for prisoners to sleep on; and if by any means they get a little, it is not changed for months together, so that it is offensive and almost worn to dust.

Few prisons separate men and women in the daytime. In some counties the gaol is also the bridewell; in others those prisons are contiguous and the courtyard common. There the petty offender is committed for instruction to the most profligate. In

For minor offenses, prisoners in the eighteenth century were put into stocks, where gathering crowds tormented them. Early colonists brought this custom to New England.

some gaols you see boys of twelve or fourteen eagerly listening to the stories told by practiced and experienced criminals, of their adventures, successes, stratagems, and escapes.

I must add that in some few gaols are confined idiots and lunatics. These serve for sport to idle visitants at assizes, and other times of general resort. Many of the bridewells are crowded and offensive, because the rooms which were designed for prisoners are occupied by the insane. Where these are not kept separate they disturb and terrify other prisoners.

Debtors crowd the gaols (especially in London) with their wives and children . . . increasing the danger of infection, and corrupting the morals of the children.

31

CORRESPONDENCE OF BENJAMIN FRANKLIN

1770

In 1770 Benjamin Franklin, the first American to win a worldwide reputation, had come to London as an agent for the hard-pressed colonies. In his letter to Monsieur Dubourg, the translator into French of Franklin's more philosophical works, he raised the question of taxation without representation, which was to become the battle cry of the mutinous colonials in their struggle with the British Empire. An eminently calm and just man, Franklin continued to believe in the triumph of reason in spite of the rising passions that were motivating both the Americans and the British.

TO M. DUBOURG

(translator of Mr. Franklin's Philosophical Works into French)

London, Oct. 2, 1770

I see with pleasure that we think pretty much alike on the subjects of English America. We of the colonies have never insisted that we ought to be exempt from contributing to the common expenses necessary to support the prosperity of the empire. We only assert that having parliaments of our own, and not having representatives in that of Gt. Britain, our parliaments are the only judges of what we can and what we ought to contribute in this case; and that the English parliament has no right to take our money without our consent. In fact, the British Empire is not a single state, it comprehends many; and though the parliament of Great Britain has arrogated to itself the power of taxing the colonies, it has no more right to do so, than it has to tax Hanover. We have the same king, but not the same legislature.

The dispute between the two countries has already lost England many millions sterling, which it has lost in its commerce, and America has in this respect been a proportionable gainer. This commerce consisted principally of superfluities; objects of luxury and fashion, which we can well do without; and the resolution we have formed of importing no more till our grievances are redressed, has enabled many of our infant manufacturers to take root; and it will not be easy to make our people abandon them in future, even should a connexion more cordial than ever succeed the present troubles. I have, indeed, no doubt that the parliament of England will finally abandon its present pretensions, and leave us to the peaceable enjoyment of our rights and privileges.

B. Franklin

32

REVOLT OF THE PROVINCIALS

1773-1783

Sir Horace Walpole, Earl of Orford, youngest son of Sir Robert Walpole, was the first Englishman to be given the title of prime minister.

Educated at Eton and Cambridge, Horace Walpole became famous as a writer, especially for his diaries, which extended from 1750 to 1787—a critical period in both English and American history. In these diaries he recorded all the crucial occurrences in the political England of his time. His estimate of men and events was both perceptive and sound.

In the excerpts that follow, Walpole begins with an English version of the Boston Tea Party and ends with an outspoken condemnation of England's "rash perseverance in a hopeless project."

THE REVOLT OF THE PROVINCIALS

by Horace Walpole

1773, June 18th.—Arrived from Boston resolutions, voted by the town of Gorham on their grievances, in which in the most open terms they disclaim the authority of Great Britain to tax them, cry out, as all men did, on the corruption of that assembly, and with reason, and declare their option of risking their lives and fortunes in defence of their rights civil and religious, rather than dying piecemeal in slavery. Corruption smiled, and was not afraid of swords at such a distance.

1774 January 18th.—This week came accounts of very riotous proceedings at Boston, where the mob broke into the ships that had brought teas, and threw about 340 chests into the sea.

August.—The month opened with very unpromising news from America. The assembly at Boston was very firm, and declaring against making composition [compensation] for the teas, was dissolved by General Gage. So was that of New Hampshire by Governor Wentworth. Several towns entered into a solemn league and covenant not to trade with Great Britain, unless the majority of the colonies should think it necessary. General Gage issued a proclamation against this covenant, declaring it illegal and hostile. At New York they burnt the effigies of Lord North, Wedderburn and Governor Hutchinson; but what was more to their purpose, they persuaded 500 of the new landed soldiers to desert, an event that had been foretold here. On this it was resolved to send over more regiments.

December 6th.—On the days of voting the army and navy there were lively debates, for the navy being lessened, though appearances were so hostile on both sides in America. Burke made a great figure, ridiculing with the highest wit and humour the inconsistency of the Ministers, their violent attack on America, followed by the contemptible inactivity of Gage, cooped up and besieged in Boston which he was sent to punish.

New edge was given to these attacks by the arrival of the long-intended sloop with the result of the American Congress, which far outwent the utmost the Ministers had feared. They flattered themselves that the colonies would submit: then that the Bostonians would offer compensation. As last they had hoped the colonies, at least the deputies, would disagree, and that at most a non-importation would be voted and not observed. Now the contrary of all this appeared. They had been unanimous, had voted non-importation, non-exportation too, and non-consumption; had voted to sell cargoes of ships bringing goods from England; had determined to support by arms such of their brothers as should be attacked; insisted on repeal of all late Acts against America, and not to submit till that was obtained,

This intelligence threw the Administration into the utmost dismay and consternation, as well it might.

1775, May 28th.—Arrived a light sloop sent by the Americans from Salem, with an account of their having defeated the King's troops. General Gage had sent a party to seize a magazine belonging to the provincials at Concord, which was guarded by militia of the province in arms. The regulars, about 1,000, attacked the provincials, not half so many, who repulsed them, and the latter retired to Lexington. The country came in to support the provincials, who lost about 50 men, and the regulars 150. The provincials had behaved with the greatest conduct, coolness, and resolution. Thus was the civil war begun, and a victory the first fruits of it on the side of the Americans, whom Lord Sandwich had had the folly and rashness to proclaim cowards.

June.—The action at Concord flew like wildfire, and threw the whole Continent into a flame. The mob rose at New York, seized, unloaded, and destroyed the cargoes of two ships lying there with provisions for Gage; and then seized a fort garrisoned by an hundred invalids, Troops from every quarter marched towards Boston, and 18,000 men invested the town. Ten thousand more were said to be on the march from Rhode Island,

A strong Remonstrance to the King in favour of America was voted with scarce a negative, and voted that it should not be delivered unless to the King *on his throne.*

July 24th.—In France, whither I went now, I did not find a single person who did not condemn our conduct towards America, our folly and cruelty. The Bishop of Mirepoix said to me, "*Vous êtes devenus fous, vous y perdrez.*"

The Congress at Philadelphia took the most resolute measures. They named Washington, a very able officer, General-in-Chief. They voted him £2,000 a year and £5 a-day for his table: he would accept only the latter.

The Provincial Congress determined on defence, formed an Union of the Twelve Provinces, chose Hancock their president, made Dr. Franklin postmaster, and sent over a firm but decent petition to the King, to which no answer was given.

1776—The year began with mighty preparations for carrying on the war in America with vigour. Lord George Sackville Germaine, who had been brought into power for that end was indefatigable in laying plans for raising and hiring troops, in sending supplies and recruits, and more naval force. Sixteen thousand Hessians were obtained, some Brunswickers, and a few other German troops. Every effort was used in these islands to raise soldiers and sailors but with indifferent success.

Feb.—At the end of the month was published a pamphlet that made a great sensation. It was called "An Essay On Civil Liberty," and was written by a Dissenter. It was a defence of the Americans, and maintained the impossibility of subduing them.

1777 Feb. 24th.—Letters from General Howe with many bad accounts and confirmation of a large body of Hessians made prisoners. The Court owned to the number of 700, but it was thought to be double. They had not been surprised, yet laid down their arms; and now began what had been for[e]seen, that the German mercenaries, whose pay was wretched and service hard and hopeless, would be seduced by their countrymen settled in America.

Dec. 1st.—At night came an express from General Carleton informing that he had learnt by deserters, and believed, that the Provincials had taken Burgoyne and his whole army prisoners. The King fell into agonies on hearing this account, but the next morning, at his levee, to disguise his concern, affected to laugh and to be so indecently merry, that Lord North endeavoured to stop him.

15th.—Arrived Captain Craig from Burgoyne, with the confirmation of the surrender of Burgoyne and the army, after great slaughter and desertion of the Germans. Burgoyne's account was in his usual bombast and absurd style; he talked of having *dic-*

tated the terms of his surrender. The terms were singularly gentle and the Provincials, while the prisoners deposited their arms, kept out of sight not to insult their disgrace.

1780. September.—Reports that General Clinton was returned to New York, not having been able to bring Washington to a battle and finding him too strongly entrenched. Thus the recovery of America, which had been promised, again vanished.

1781. Nov. 3rd.—Colonel Robert Conway, aide-de-camp to Sir H. Clinton, arrived express from him to represent the desperate posture of affairs. Lord Cornwallis was in most imminent danger of being enveloped and starved by the Americans and French, the latter having landed 4,000 men, and Lord Cornwallis having provisions but for a month or six weeks.

25th. A packet-boat that had carried the Compte de Jarnac from Dover to Calais brought back a French "Gazette," with an account of Lord Cornwallis and his whole army having been made prisoners at York Town by General Washington, at the head of the French and Americans. This was soon confirmed by an express from Sir Henry Clinton.

This news threw the Court and Administration into great confusion and distress.

1782. Jan.—The Court began the year in great perplexity. The defeat of Lord Cornwallis and the capture of his army had rendered the American war hopeless; yet the King was not in the least more inclined to give up.

Feb. 27th.—The decisive blow was given to an Administration which had given the most fatal stab to the glory and interests of England, by (I believe) planning (certainly by taking no step to prevent), pushing on, and persisting in the American war, and who had maintained themselves under the greatest disgraces and losses that ever this country had sustained—disgraces in a great measure the consequence of impolicy, early neglect, and rash perseverance in a hopeless project.

1783. Jan. 21st.—The Parliament met again after the recess. As the account of the Preliminaries of Peace being signed at Paris was every moment expected, the Opposition lay by and would not say a word. 22nd.—Bill brought in for ceding all control of England over Ireland. 23d.—At last, in the evening, courier arrived with account of the Preliminaries being signed by France, Spain and America. Thus in one week the King gave up all control over Ireland, and the total sovereignty of North America, by grasping at despotism over which he lost both America and Ireland! What a lesson to despotic ambition—if ambition would learn from example!

33

WILLIAM PITT SPEAKS OUT

1774

The thirteen American colonies stretched for a distance of seventeen hundred miles along the Atlantic Coast from Massachusetts to Georgia. Although the colonies differed widely between themselves on many issues, they were united by the proud love of liberty that has been basic to the English character since the days of the Magna Charta. The colonies also shared a common indignation against what they regarded as the unfair "taxation without representation" that had been imposed on them by the mother country.

In England, William Pitt, who was known as the Great Commoner, opposed the government's shortsighted American policy. The colonists looked on him as their greatest and most powerful friend in the home government. When Fort Duquesne was rebuilt, they named it Fort Pitt in his honor. Later the city that grew up on that site became "Pittsburgh."

SPEECH ON THE AMERICAN WAR OF INDEPENDENCE

by William Pitt

My Lords . . . If we take a transient view of those motives which induced the ancestors of our fellow-subjects in America to leave their native country, to encounter the innumerable difficulties in the unexplored regions of the western world, our astonishment of the present conduct of their descendants will naturally subside. There was no corner of the world into which men of their free and enterprising spirit would not fly with alacrity, rather than submit to the slavish and tyrannical principles, which prevailed at that period in their native country. And shall we wonder, my Lords, if the descendants of such illustrious characters spurn, with contempt, the hand of unconstitutional power, that would snatch from them such dear-bought privileges as they now contend for? Had the British Colonies been planted by any other kingdom than our own, the inhabitants would have carried with them the chains of slavery, and spirit of despotism; but as they are, they ought to be remembered as great instances to instruct the world what great exertions mankind will naturally make, when they are left to the free exercise of their own powers. And, my Lords, notwithstanding my intention to give my hearty negative to the question now before you [a bill for quartering British soldiers in America], I cannot help condemning, in the severest manner, the late turbulent and unwarrantable conduct of the Americans in some instances, particularly in the late riots of Boston. But, my Lords, the mode which has been pursued to bring them back to a sense of their duty to their parent state has been diametrically opposite to the fundamental principles of sound policy. . . . By blocking up the harbour of Boston, you have involved the innocent trader in the same punishment with the guilty profligates who destroyed your merchandise; and instead of making a well-concerted effort to secure the real offenders, you clap a military and naval extinguisher over their harbor. . . .

My Lords, the country is little obliged to the framers and promoters of this tea-tax. The Americans had almost forgot, in their excess of gratitude for the repeal of the stamp act, any interest but that of the mother country; there seemed an emulation among the different provinces, who should be most dutiful and forward in their expressions of loyalty. But the moment they perceived your intention was renewed to tax them, under a pretense of serving the East India Company, their resentment got the ascendant of their moderation, and hurried them into actions contrary to law, which, in their cooler hours, they would have thought on with horror; for I sincerely believe, the destroying of the tea was the effect of despair.

But my Lords, from the complexion of the whole of the proceedings, I think the administration has purposely irritated them into those violent acts for which they now so severely smart; purposely to be revenged on them for the victory they gained by the repeal of the stamp act. For what other motive could induce them to dress taxation, that father of American sedition, in the robes of an East India Director, but to break in upon that mutual peace and harmony. . . .

My Lords, I am an old man, and would advise the noble Lords in office to adopt a more gentle mode of governing America . . .

This, my Lords, though no new doctrine, has always been my unalterable opinion, and I will carry it to my grave, *that this country had no right under heaven to tax America.* It is contrary to all the principles of justice and civil policy. Such proceedings will never meet their wished-for success; and, instead of adding to their miseries, as the bill now before you most undoubtedly does, adopt some lenient measures, which may lure them to their duty; proceed like a kind and affectionate parent over a child whom he tenderly loves; and, instead of those harsh and severe proceedings pass an amnesty on all their youthful errors; clasp them once more in your fond and affectionate arms; and I will venture to affirm you will find them children worthy of their sire.

34

THE HALCYON DAYS OF OLD ENGLAND

1778

The "broadside" originated in England. Usually consisting of a single sheet of paper printed on only one side, it was frequently used as a convenient means for the dissemination of political opinions.

"The Halcyon Days of Old England" is a good example of this type of political propaganda. Horace Walpole relished it and copied it into his diary. It is an example of the existence of an active antiwar faction during the height of the unpopular colonial war.

THE HALCYON DAYS OF OLD ENGLAND

OR

Wisdom of Administration Demonstrated

A BALLAD

To the tune of 'Ye Medley of Mortals.'

Give ear to my song, I'll now tell you a story,
This is the bright era of Old England's glory;
And though some may think us in pitiful plight,
I'll swear they're mistaken, for matters go right!
Sing tantarara, wise all.
Sing tantarara, wise all, wise all,

Let us laugh at the cavils of weak silly elves!
Our statesmen are wise men!—they say so themselves!
And though little mortals may hear it with wonder,
'Tis consummate wisdom that causes each blunder!
REFRAIN: "*Sing tantarara, . . .*"

They now are conducting a glorious war!
(It began about tea, about feathers, and tar!)
With spirit they pushed what they planned with sense!
Forty millions they've spent for a tax of threepence!
REFRAIN: "*Sing tantarara, . . .*"

The debts of this nation do grieve them so sore,
To lighten our burden—they load us the more!
They aim at th' American's cash, my dear honey!
Yet beggar this kingdom and send them the money.
REFRAIN: "*Sing tantarara, . . .*"

What honors we're gaining by taking their forts,
Destroying batteaux and blocking up ports;
Burgoyne would have worked them—but for a mishap,
By Gates and one Arnold he'd caught in a trap!
REFRAIN: "*Sing tantarara, . . .*"

But Howe was more cautious and prudent by far,
He sailed with his fleet up the great Delaware;
All summer he struggled and strove to undo them,
But the plague of it was that he could not get to them.
    REFRAIN: "*Sing tantarara, . . .*"

Oh think us not cruel because our allies
Are savagely scalping men, women, and boys!
Maternal affection to this step doth move us—
The more they are scalped, the more they will love us!
    REFRAIN: "*Sing tantarara, . . .*"

Some folks are uneasy and make a great pother,
For the loss of one army and half of another:
But sirs, next campaign by ten thousands we'll slay them!
If we can find soldiers and money to pay them!
    REFRAIN: "*Sing tantarara, . . .*"

I've sung you my song, now I'll give you a pray'r:
May peace soon succeed to this horrible war!
Again may we live with our brethren in concord!
And the authors of mischief all hang in a strong cord!
    REFRAIN: "*Sing tantarara, . . .*"

INDEX